North Warwickshire & Hinckley College Library

Good learners become great

.ac.uk

CHANDOS
INFORMATION PROFESSIONAL SERIES

Series Editor: Ruth Rikowski
(email: Rikowskigr@aol.com)

Chandos' new series of books are aimed at the busy information professional. They have been specially commissioned to provide the reader with an authoritative view of current thinking. They are designed to provide easy-to-read and (most importantly) practical coverage of topics that are of interest to librarians and other information professionals. If you would like a full listing of current and forthcoming titles, please visit our web site **www.chandospublishing.com** or contact Hannah Grace-Williams on email info@chandospublishing.com or telephone number +44 (0) 1993 848726.

New authors: we are always pleased to receive ideas for new titles; if you would like to write a book for Chandos, please contact Dr Glyn Jones on email gjones@chandospublishing.com or telephone number +44 (0) 1993 848726.

Bulk orders: some organisations buy a number of copies of our books. If you are interested in doing this, we would be pleased to discuss a discount. Please contact Hannah Grace-Williams on email info@chandospublishing.com or telephone number +44 (0) 1993 848726.

Joint-use Libraries:
Libraries for the future

SARAH MCNICOL

Chandos Publishing

Oxford · England

Chandos Publishing (Oxford) Limited
TBAC Business Centre
Avenue 4
Station Lane
Witney
Oxford OX28 4BN
UK
Tel: +44 (0) 1993 848726 Fax: +44 (0) 1865 884448
Email: info@chandospublishing.com
www.chandospublishing.com

First published in Great Britain in 2008

ISBN:
978 1 84334 384 4 (paperback)
978 1 84334 385 1 (hardback)
1 84334 384 3 (paperback)
1 84334 385 1 (hardback)

© S. McNicol, 2008

British Library Cataloguing-in-Publication Data.
A catalogue record for this book is available from the British Library.

Typeset by Domex e-Data Pvt. Ltd.
Printed in the UK by 4edge Ltd, Hockley. www.4edge.co.uk

Contents

List of figures and table

Figures

Table

About the author

Sarah McNicol has worked as a researcher in the library and information field in the UK since 2000. She is based at Evidence Base, a research and evaluation unit at Birmingham City University, UK, and has worked on over 30 projects, both large and small scale.

In June 2007 she organised the first international conference on joint-use libraries; this was attended by more than 100 delegates from Europe, North America and Australasia. Her research into joint-use libraries includes various surveys and case studies in the UK and overseas. In 2006 she guest edited a special edition of *Library Trends* on joint-use libraries.

Apart from joint-use libraries, her main research interests are school libraries, children's services, censorship and lifelong learning, and she has written and presented extensively on these and other topics. Before moving into research, she previously worked as a school librarian for six years.

Acknowledgements

I would like to thank all the contributors to the first international joint-use libraries conference which was held in Manchester, UK, in June 2007. I have drawn heavily on the papers presented at this conference to provide details of the latest developments in joint-use libraries around the world. I would also like to thank the following people who provided additional information which was valuable in the writing of this book: Guy Cotton from Galliford Try Investments, Jodi McLaughlin from Dalhousie University, Canada, Craig Green and Fiona McLelland from The Bridge in Glasgow and Jackson Ndlovu from the Natural History Museum in Zimbabwe.

Photographs were provided by Harriett MacDougall, Alvin Sherman Library, Research, and Information Technology Center; Sonia Sumner, Alice Springs Campus, Charles Darwin University; and Suzan R. Edwards, Harley Ellis Devereaux.

List of acronyms

ACE	Advanced Certificate in Education
ALA	American Library Association
ALIA	Australian Library and Information Association
CAB	Citizens Advice Bureau
CCLA	College Center for Library Automation
CILIP	Chartered Institute of Library and Information Professionals (UK)
CMU	concrete masonry unit
CSAP	Colorado Student Assessment Program
CSC	customer service centre
CSF	critical success factor
DBCC	Daytona Beach Community College
DfES	Department for Education and Skills (UK)
DQI	Design Quality Indicators
EBLIDA	European Bureau of Library, Information and Documentation Associations
EIS	electronic information services
ESL	English as a second language
HE	higher education
HEFCE	Higher Education Funding Council for England
HEI	higher education institution
ICT	information and communication technology
IFLA	International Federation of Library Associations and Institutions
ISBN	International Standard Book Number
ISSN	International Standard Serial Number

JISC	Joint Information Systems Committee
LGBT	lesbians, gay men, bisexuals and transgendered people
LIC	Library and Information Commission (UK)
LM	library media
LMC	library media centre
LMS	library media specialist
LRC	learning resource centre
LSC	Learning and Skills Council (UK)
MLA	Museums, Libraries and Archives Council (UK)
NCLIS	National Commission on Libraries and Information Science (USA)
NHS	National Health Service (UK)
NIH	National Institutes of Health (USA)
NLM	National Library of Medicine (USA)
NT	Northern Territory (Australia)
Pals	Patient Advice and Liaison Service
PANDA	Pickering and Newington Development Association
PC	personal computer
PCT	Primary Care Trust
PFI	Private Finance Initiative
PLQIM	Public Library Quality Improvement Matrix
RIBA	Royal Institute of British Architects
SCONUL	Society of College, National and University Libraries (UK)
SLA	School Library Association (UK)
TAFE	technical and further education
TIC	tourist information centre
TUPE	Transfer of Undertakings (Protection of Employment) Regulations
UCF	University of Central Florida
UCLAN	University of Central Lancashire

UHI	University of the Highlands and Islands
UNESCO	UN Economic, Social and Cultural Organization
VET	vocational education and training
WEA	Workers' Educational Association (UK)
ZIB	Zentrum für Information und Bildung

Introduction

For many years joint-use libraries have been the Cinderella of the library sector. They were criticised and derided by many in the profession as an inferior form of library provision. However, after more than 100 years, it seems as though in the early twenty-first century they are finally coming into their own. Perhaps more than any other type of library, joint-use services are ideally suited to the current political climate and drivers for change in society. They encourage collaboration and partnership working; they can be a more efficient means of providing services; they have the potential to be more environmentally sustainable; they can be a forum to promote lifelong learning, especially within communities where education has not been traditionally valued; and, perhaps most importantly of all, they can help to combat social exclusion and promote community cohesion, creating a more equitable society.

This book examines the current state of knowledge about joint-use libraries and considers why they are so important to the future of the library profession as a whole. Joint-use libraries have been in existence for many years, but over the last two decades their number has been growing at an ever-increasing rate. For example, in 1978 there were just 21 joint-use libraries reported in Australia, but by 2007 the number had risen to 120 (Bundy, 2007). The total number of joint-use libraries in many other countries is unknown, but numerous examples can be found in Africa, Asia and South America as well as Europe, the USA and Australasia.

Given their long history, it may seem somewhat belated to talk about joint-use libraries as 'libraries for the future', but not only do they correspond to contemporary policy initiatives and social concerns such as inclusion, lifelong learning, collaboration and social equality, they also contribute to debates within the library profession about the future of library services in the face of issues such as falling visitor numbers, poor-quality building stock and, for some, a low profile within their wider organisation or community. This means that greater knowledge of joint-use libraries is not only of benefit to those within this sector, but elements can be applicable to most, if not all, single-sector libraries too. In particular, joint-use library staff are developing innovative models of service provision, new types of partnership working and novel ways of engaging with users and non-users. The results of their explorations are extremely valuable for the profession as a whole. It is therefore vital that joint-use libraries are not marginalised, but seen as credible forms of library provision which can provide models, ideas and inspiration – not only among other joint-use librarians, but much more widely. Hopefully, this book will be of interest not just to those directly concerned with joint-use libraries, but also to those whose primary interests lie elsewhere, such as in supporting lifelong learning, community cohesion, social justice or partnership working.

Outline of the book

Although joint-use libraries have gained a much higher profile in the last few years, 'What exactly is a joint-use library?' is a question that is still frequently asked, even within the library profession. Chapter 1 therefore attempts to answer this question, setting out a definition of joint-use libraries, or at least one which applies for the scope of this book. Historically, joint-use libraries have widely been regarded as synonymous with the terms 'dual-use libraries' and 'school-community libraries', but this has now changed. Today, the types of joint-use library and partnership combinations are considerably more varied: there are significant numbers of college-public, university-public, health-public and health-university libraries, to give just a few examples. There are also tripartite libraries, and libraries which have joined with other information services to create one-stop shops. And, increasingly, libraries are becoming part of multipurpose centres where they are co-located with other types of service such as leisure facilities, health centres or community centres. No doubt, in the next few years, even more examples will emerge.

Chapter 2 considers why a joint-use library might be considered a viable form of library provision within a particular community. The ethos of most joint-use libraries chimes with the broad concerns of the library profession to build a democratic society by improving access to a wide range of information and ideas and combating social exclusion to create a more equal society. However, there are also more pragmatic reasons why the number of joint-use libraries is increasing, including drives for greater efficiency and economy in the delivery of public services, changing organisational structures and demographic trends. In the last decade, in the UK in particular, the development of joint-use libraries has also indirectly been supported by a number of government policy initiatives which have encouraged collaboration, efficiency and 'joined-up' public services.

Some joint-use libraries are purpose-designed new builds, while others have to make the best use of existing buildings. The design of a joint-use library is the subject of Chapter 3. Here, a number of key features are discussed, such as location, access, signposting, layout and interior design. Case studies highlight how space can be used to cater for the needs of differing user groups; the use of art to create an impact; the importance of user consultation; and sustainable design, a consideration which is likely to become more and more important over the next few years.

Chapter 4 looks at how a joint-use library can operate effectively. This includes the service-level agreement, governance and management structures, communications, budgeting, staffing, collection development, technology and access arrangements. In smaller school-community libraries many of these issues can be resolved relatively easily, but as larger organisations and multiple partners are increasingly involved in joint-use libraries, establishing an effective way of functioning, both at a strategic level and on a day-to-day basis, is ever more important. The examples given in this chapter describe some of the ways these issues have been addressed by existing joint-use libraries. The overwhelming message is that the key to success is compromise and the capacity for change. In many instances the best solution is not the approach adopted by one type of library service or another, but an entirely new way of working.

Partnerships are, of course, at the heart of any joint-use library, and this is discussed in Chapter 5. It is perhaps in this area that joint-use librarians have the most to share with their colleagues in other library services. Joint-use libraries work with a vast range of partners and, over a number of years, much has been learnt about the opportunities offered by these partnerships; what difficulties they face and how these can be overcome; and what factors make for a successful partnership. As libraries in all sectors are facing mounting pressure to work more collaboratively, joint-use librarians have much to offer the wider profession through sharing their experiences.

Of course, one essential partner in any joint-use library is its user community. Chapter 6 considers the role of joint-use libraries in supporting social inclusion and community cohesion. By widening access to resources, joint-use libraries can help to reduce divisions within society. Traditionally, joint-use school-community libraries have helped to provide better library services to isolated rural communities. However, joint-use libraries are increasingly finding ways to support other groups which many libraries find hard to reach, such as ethnic minority communities. Central to this are community engagement activities such as information-gathering, consultation and participation.

Another area where joint-use libraries can make a significant contribution is in expanding the horizons of both library staff and users. In particular, as described in Chapter 7, they support the notion of lifelong learning by creating links between informal and formal learning providers. The development of 'learning centres' is a notable example of the trend to establish joint facilities linking library and information services and learning providers, but joint-use libraries can also support learning in other ways, including literacy initiatives for both children and adults, information literacy training for users and intergenerational learning projects.

Chapter 8 asks 'How good are joint-use libraries? (And how do we know?)'. One issue which needs to be addressed if joint-use libraries are to be promoted more assertively to those outside the sector is the current lack of evaluation of joint-use libraries and the need for more robust evidence of their effectiveness and impact. This chapter describes the evaluation model devised for joint-use libraries by Larry Amey in the 1980s, which he revised in 2006 with Alan Bundy. It also considers models from other sectors which may be relevant to evaluate the partnership elements of a joint-use library, and looks at the applicability of standards and checklists to help joint-use library staff to monitor their services.

Finally, Chapter 9 looks at the future for joint-use libraries.

Hopefully this book will be of use not just to those working in all types of joint-use libraries, but to anyone interested in the potential of new models of library provision to meet the changing needs of library users, and potential users, in the twenty-first century.

What are joint-use libraries?

Joint-use libraries, along with co-located libraries and shared services, seem to be increasingly prevalent across all library sectors. Alongside high-profile projects such as the Dr Martin Luther King Jr Library in San José in California and the planned joint-use library and local history centre in Worcester in the UK, there are dozens of smaller-scale projects being initiated, often as a result of the growing pressure for cross-sectoral cooperation emanating from governments and other policy-makers.

A widely accepted definition of joint-use libraries is '...outcomes of formal agreements between two or more separate authorities which provide two or more groups of users with equitable access to resources, services and facilities' (Bundy, 1997: 1). The broadness of this definition hints at the variety of models of joint-use library provision which now exist around the world. Just a few of the numerous types are school-community libraries, university-community libraries, college-university libraries, college-community libraries, government-university libraries, health-university libraries, research-business libraries, council information-community libraries, children's information-community libraries, health information-community libraries and tourist information-community libraries. Although most joint-use libraries are based on an agreement between two partners, multiple-partnership libraries are becoming increasingly common – for example, university-college-public libraries and university-college-school libraries. Joint-use libraries are indeed 'libraries like no other' (SJLibrary.org, 2007a), and it has been argued that they should be regarded as new form of library with a unique identity (Hansson, 2006).

The origins of joint-use libraries

Joint-use libraries are not a new phenomenon; they have existed around the world for more than a century. School-housed public libraries date back to at least 1906, with one having operated continuously in New Hampshire in the USA since then. The first South Australian school-community library was founded in 1856, and the earliest formal Australian proposal for a system of school-community libraries was made by the Queensland State Department of Public Instruction in 1909. During the first half of the twentieth century, before public libraries were developed in Australia, school libraries sometimes made their resources available to parents and the local community. In Sweden there have been examples of combined parish-school libraries since the mid-nineteenth century. James Kay Shuttleworth was an early advocate of fusing school and public libraries in Britain. In 1840 he argued that 'The parochial or village library can nowhere be so conveniently and usefully kept as at the school house under the charge of the school-master' (Minutes of the Privy Council Committee for Education, 20 February 1840, quoted in Jones, 1977: 311).

This concept was developed by Henry Morris in the 1920s and 1930s: he created colleges in Cambridgeshire which combined a school with facilities for adult education and community activities. In the late 1940s there were proposals for community colleges in Leicestershire which would feature a public library shared with a school. But to put the scale of UK joint-use library provision into perspective, in 1970 there were just ten to 15 dual-purpose libraries, mostly in schools and usually accommodated in existing school premises – for example, a converted classroom. During the next five years the number doubled, but they were still a rarity (Jones, 1977).

The spread of joint-use libraries

Today, the total number of joint-use libraries is unknown. In 2000 Fitzgibbons reported at least 67 joint-use libraries in 17 states in the USA. The largest numbers were in Vermont (12), Alaska (ten) and Kansas (eight). In the 1970s there were 179 school-community libraries included in Amey's (1979) survey in Canada; and in Australia the number of joint-use libraries rose from 21 in 1978 to 44 in 1983 and approximately 120 in 2007 (Bundy, 2007). A survey sent to all UK public library authorities in 2005 reported 60 joint-use libraries, but this is certainly an underestimate even of merely those joint-use libraries with a public library component. 'Start with the child' reported that:

> Links between schools and their local public library continue although there is a lack of published evidence to show trends. Dual use libraries are still being built or established. Best Value and the need to provide libraries in a bigger range of locations appear to be revitalising this approach. (CILIP, 2002b: 64)

And the extent of joint-use libraries in other countries is even less certain, and the number of co-located libraries even more unclear.

Although joint-use libraries are best documented in North America, Australasia and parts of Europe, examples can be found around the world. For example, the Provincial Medical Documentation and Information Centre in China is a joint academic library and information institute. Also, in China's Shandong province, the Liaocheng Teachers' College and Liaocheng city have built a joint-use library which serves as an academic library and city public library. There are also a number of examples in Africa, some of which are described in Chapter 9.

Models of joint-use libraries

The opening chapters of this book consider what exactly a joint-use library is in terms of its conception, design, organisation and management. An interesting point is raised by Zetterlund and Garden (2007), who make the distinction between the administrative and conceptual, or ideological, perspectives of joint-use libraries. While the administrative perspective relates to cooperation to produce shared services, the conceptual perspective relates to the integration of certain basic ideas emanating from different types of library.

So, are joint-use libraries simply convenient administrative arrangements, or something more? And does the creation of a joint-use library offer something extra, above what would have been provided by two individual libraries? A number of commentators have developed models of joint-use provision. The following are just a few examples.

Reflecting on cooperation between public libraries and schools in Canada, Sandra Morden (2003) described three different models.

- *Independent shared site.* This is not a shared library but, for example, a public library located on or near school property. The school and public library are separate buildings and each has its own entrance. The school and library are run independently, but the public library may pay rent for the land. However, this type of library can be considered joint use because the school uses the library as its own library. Some variations on this model include:
  - the school may have an additional entrance to the library from inside the school building;
  - there may be a small shared space, such as a PC lab;
  - the school may also have its own library within the school;
  - the public library may provide some services to the school, for example a shared student/public library card.

- *One space, public library provides all the services.* There is a single library for the public and the school. The majority of the collection is provided by the public library, although a small collection may be added by the school. The library may have shared or separate entrances for public and school users. Although the public library provides all the library services, the school might contribute, for example by providing a computer lab which is available to the public after school hours. The public library may charge the school a fee for the services and staffing it provides. There may be some variation on this model – for example, the school and public library may be in separate buildings, or form part of a larger complex.

- *One space, division of responsibilities and control.* There is one shared library for the public and school and a combined collection, although school materials may be a small part of the total collection. Typically, the public library provides information and circulation services. School staff are usually responsible for students during schools hours, and the school may provide services such as cleaning and maintenance. There is usually additional shared space, such as meeting rooms. The school normally provides a computer lab which is available to the public after school hours, in addition to the public library's PCs. The management committee has representatives from both school and public library, and costs are divided proportionally according to a formula as set out in a written agreement. Alternatively, a formula of services and fees may be set up. Variations on this model include:

— separate service points for students during the school day;

— some segregated areas;

— the school may provide staffing;

— cataloguing/circulation systems may be provided by the school.

An alternative framework was presented by the Queensland Government (2005), which set out options for cooperation and partnership between school and community libraries. The alternative forms of cooperation are:

- school resource centre offering some community services without any input from public library authority *or* public library offering some curriculum-oriented services without input from school;

- school offering some community services with minimal input from public library, or vice versa;

- joint-use library provided by one partner, with significant input from the other;

- joint-use library on either school or local government premises provided on the basis of fully shared input from education and public library authorities;
- joint-use library on third-party premises provided on the basis of fully shared input from education and public library authorities;
- community library integrated as part of a complex of education, health, social welfare, recreation and cultural facilities.

Karen Dornseif (2001) identified three levels of integration to create yet another model.

- *Minimal integration* – libraries are co-located, but preserve their individual identities and services.
- *Selective integration* – each partner brings its own specific strengths to the collaboration.
- *Full integration* – libraries have a shared mission.

While these models are undoubtedly useful, the importance of relationships in any collaborative venture suggests that injecting a more 'human' element might provide an alternative way of thinking about the forms of joint-use libraries. Of course, there is overlap between these categories, and individual libraries may incorporate elements from more than one of the 'relationship' types described below.

The lodger

One partner is, essentially, a lodger in the other's premises, having little or no say in how the other operates. They share a building, but are likely to have their own defined space and, to a large extent, operate entirely separately.

Example: Furzebank Library, Willenhall school sports college, Walsall, UK

Furzebank Library was opened at the same time as the Willenhall school, in the late 1970s. Prior to its recent closure after almost 30 years, it was located at the side of the main school building, but was not well signed either from the road or within the school grounds. All the staff at Furzebank were employed by Walsall public library service. All resources were purchased by the public library; there was no school-book budget for the library. There was limited contact between the head teacher and library staff. Library staff felt that those teachers who did make regular use of the library valued its services, but many did not use it or were not fully aware of what it could offer. Although adult education classes were held at the school, these made little impact on the work of the library (McNicol, 2003).

The flatmates

The partners share responsibility for the management and operation of the service and agree how each will make a comparable contribution to the resourcing and running of the library. They share some resources and services, but preserve a degree of independence from each other – for instance, separate ICT networks and separate staffing structures.

Example: Metropolitan State University St Paul Campus in Minnesota

Here, a key agreement at the outset was that this would not be a merged library operation. Each organisation would maintain its own identity, staffing, materials, programmes of service and so forth. The entire library serves all users, but a specific section of the building is operated by the public library system in much the same way as any other branch library.

The marriage

The services are fully integrated, sharing collections, staffing, space, issuing systems etc.

Example: The Bridge, Glasgow, UK

The Bridge is an example of a full-integration joint-use library model which includes joint use of buildings, co-location of services and a merged college/public library service. Each partner plays to its strengths. The public library service, Culture and Sport Glasgow, has responsibility for delivering library services to both the public and college students and staff, while John Wheatley College has responsibility for delivery of learning support services to the local population.

The key features of the merged college/public library service are:

- the physical merging of the college and public library facilities;
- the transfer of college library staff to the employment of the council and college 'buy back' of library services;
- the allocation of responsibility for ICT service delivery for both communities to the college;
- the production of a legally binding service-level agreement;
- a single library management system and combined library catalogue;
- the provision of college learning support services to both communities as part of its wider community learning partnership.

Types of joint-use library facilities

As suggested above, there are already a huge variety of joint-use library partnerships and the range is expanding every year. Those described below are the most common forms of joint-use provision at present.

School-community (public) libraries

School-community libraries, or school-housed public libraries, have the longest history and are the most prevalent form of joint-use library. The published case studies and research literature on joint-use services relate mostly to these types of libraries. They are usually located on school premises, sometimes within the school itself. This raises a number of issues, including security and the reluctance of some adults to visit a school. However, many school-community libraries do provide an effective library service, especially for communities in isolated rural areas.

In recent years some interesting variations on the basic school-public library model have emerged. For instance, Le Roux and Hendrikz (2006) described a variation on the model of school-community library designed to serve remote rural areas of South Africa. Here, due to the shortage of school library facilities, the combined library is located in a public library which serves a cluster of schools within a half-mile (750 metre) radius.

In some cases, school-public joint-use libraries have focused on children's services. For example, Horwich Library in Bolton is situated across the road from a primary school and a lower secondary school annexe. In 2005 Department for Education and Skills' funding and the library service's own monies enabled the conversion of an archive storeroom at a 1930s' library into an expanded and enhanced children's and school library for the two nearby schools. A part-time library assistant from the lower secondary school library was integrated with the public library staff, although still paid for by the school. In addition, another part-time school library assistant remained at the school acting as a liaison officer between the public library and the schools to ensure that visits were timetabled and children escorted across the road to use the premises. By joining together, facilities have been improved for children in the area in a way which would have been difficult to do on stand-alone budgets within either the library service or the schools. An added benefit is that these facilities are available to children outside school time (Keane, 2007).

Other education-public joint-use libraries

In 2001 joint-use academic-public libraries were identified as the fastest-growing trend along with community college-university libraries (Miller and Pellen, 2001). Since 1990 there have been major joint university-public libraries developed in Australia, Finland, Latvia, Sweden and the USA. The number of shared college-public library facilities has also risen in recent years. The largest such development is the $177.5 million, 475,000 square feet (44,130 square metres) King Library, which opened in 2003. This is an initiative between the city of San José and San José State University in California. Large-scale university-public libraries are now being planned elsewhere, including the UK and Mexico. While these have often been controversial, they are not a new development; Europe has a long history of shared public and university library services. For instance, the Bibliotheque Publique et Universitaire in Geneva was founded in 1559.

Example: Alvin Sherman Library, Research, and Information Technology Center, Florida, USA

The Alvin Sherman Library, Research, and Information Technology Center, which opened in 2001, is the largest library building in the state of Florida. It serves the Broward County community and the students, faculty and staff of Nova Southeastern University. The 325,000 square foot (30,190 square metres) facility combines a public library, an academic library, auditoria, classrooms and computer labs in one building. The entire library is open to all users. Services include collections of research materials, specialised databases, popular fiction and non-fiction books, magazines and journals, CDs, DVDs, special programmes for children and teenagers, book discussion groups, author readings and classes on using research tools and resources.

Joint-use libraries in educational institutions

Other examples of joint-use libraries shared between educational institutions include school-college libraries and combined primary-secondary school libraries, but by far the most common type is joint educational libraries shared between colleges and universities. For instance, there are four examples in Australia of libraries serving higher education, vocational education and school students. In Florida there are four joint-use libraries which have been developed through a partnership between the University of Central Florida and community colleges. At a less formal level, in the UK the trend to offer higher education courses from further education institutions means that many college libraries are actually functioning as joint-use libraries, although this is not officially recognised.

Example: Daytona Beach Community College/ University of Central Florida Joint-Use Library

The Daytona Beach Community College/University of Central Florida (DBCC/UCF) Joint-Use Library is a model of cooperation between two educational establishments to provide for the student, faculty and staff needs of both. The library is located on the main campus of the Daytona Beach Community College. The University of Central Florida's Daytona Beach regional campus is located in two buildings on the DBCC campus. The building also houses an open computer lab and the DBCC's Virtual College. Circulation, technical services, media, the circulating print collection and the library director's office are located on the first level. The DBCC reference computers, reference print collection and reference desk are on the second level, and the law collection, periodicals and the UCF reference computers are on the third level. Study areas are located throughout the library. Each library purchases materials for the joint-use library from separate budgets. Each institution has an acquisitions and technical services department. The reference desk is staffed by a librarian at all times that the joint-use library is open, and librarians from both institutions deal with reference enquiries from all students (Bozeman and Owens, 2007).

Health-university libraries

As Linda Dorrington (2006) pointed out, the joint use of health libraries by practitioners and students has been a recognised practice going back many years, although there is very little documentation to support it. Although these libraries are much fewer in number than the types of joint-use facility described above, they are becoming more common – for example, the new Health Library in

Stoke-on-Trent, UK, provides stock and services for the National Health Service (NHS) community in north Staffordshire and Keele University's Faculty of Health, and the Royal Blackburn Hospital Learning Centre Library in East Lancashire is a joint partnership between the East Lancashire Hospitals NHS Trust and the University of Central Lancashire (UCLAN) Library and Learning Resource Service. There are also examples of joint-use partnerships between the NHS and public libraries, including the Revive Healthy Living Centre in Derby, UK, and the link between Bolton Primary Care Trust and Bolton Libraries, UK.

Example: Health Library in Stoke-on-Trent, UK

This joint NHS-university library in north Staffordshire opened in 2004. The Health Library is a new service, based in the Clinical Education Centre at the City General Hospital in Stoke-on-Trent. It integrates the services previously provided by the North Staffordshire Medical Institute Library and the Keele Health Library. Its services are available to everyone who works for, or with, the NHS in north Staffordshire, all students and staff of Keele University and others with a need for health information.

Staff from the two libraries have merged and, over time, all will have university employment contracts. Staff believe that there are many benefits of a joint service for users. For example, the book stock for NHS staff has vastly improved and opening hours have extended considerably, while university users have access to a much wider range of journals. However, perhaps the main benefit is the fact that users now know they can go to a single location to obtain resources; they do not have to have a detailed knowledge of the resources kept in each location.

Joint university-national libraries

An interesting example of a large-scale joint-use research library is Landsbókasafn Íslands – Háskólabókasafn, which was established by the amalgamation of the National Library of Iceland and the library of the University of Iceland and opened in a new building in 1994. The Icelandic parliament had first resolved that the National Library of Iceland and the university library should be amalgamated back in 1957. This is, by far, the largest research library in Iceland. The four floors and basement cover a total of 140,000 square feet (13,000 square metres) and have a capacity for 900,000 volumes, plus seating for 700 visitors. As well as providing for the needs of teaching and research activities at the University of Iceland, the library collects all Icelandic published materials, both printed and in other formats, and makes them available to the public; provides library and information services for the benefit of industry, government and research; operates a union catalogue for Icelandic libraries; and operates the national office for the International Standard Book Number (ISBN) and International Standard Serial Number (ISSN) systems.

Joint-use digital libraries

At the beginning of the twenty-first century, it is no longer sufficient to consider joint-use libraries as those sharing physical space. Increasingly, digital libraries and websites are being designed to meet the needs of more than a single user group, through the use of differentiated entry points or portals for instance. Although this is not something considered in detail in this book, it is a trend which is likely to become more important in the future.

Interestingly, Joacim Hansson (2007) draws parallels between joint-use libraries and digital libraries, as both challenge the institutional borders of more traditional libraries which are tied to a specific university, school or other organisation.

Example: US National Library of Medicine

From its beginnings as the Library of the Army of the Surgeon General, the US National Library of Medicine (NLM) has served a variety of audiences. Over time the form of the service has changed, depending on resources available and the state of technology. Today, the NLM provides electronic biomedical information to anyone with access to the internet: health professionals, researchers and the public.

In 1993 the NLM was one of the first US agencies with a presence on the World Wide Web. The most important service from the mid-1990s was MEDLINE in its expanded form, PubMed. Anyone with internet access, from researchers to clinicians to librarians, could search MEDLINE/PubMed. Novice users searched the literature using simple keywords, while experienced librarians learned to use the advanced features for more precise or comprehensive results, depending on the needs of their clinician clients. Use of the system grew from 7 million user searches in 1997 to 2.7 million searches each day in 2004.

A 1997 survey of MEDLINE/PubMed users (reported in Lacroix and Backus, 2006: 611) showed that over 30 per cent identified themselves as members of the general public rather than as scientists, health-professionals or librarians. The NLM responded by releasing MedlinePlus.gov, a consumer health portal, to the internet in October 1998.

Both PubMed and MedlinePlus serve a variety of audiences, providing a continuum of health and biomedical information. The services are interlinked so that consumers and health professionals can move easily between the two resources. Contextual links allow users to navigate between the sites within their health topic of interest, without starting again at the beginning of their subject search. These subject-based links allow PubMed health-professional users to link easily to consumer-level information for their own background material or for a patient or family member.

The NLM uses this same approach to guide users of MedlinePlus and PubMed to ClinicalTrials.gov, a registry of over 13,000 clinical studies sponsored by the National Institutes of Health (NIH), other government agencies and private industry, and to Genetics Home Reference, the NLM's consumer health guide to understanding genetic conditions. By creating links on each of the tools, the NLM facilitates all users moving to and from basic health information, clinical trials and in-depth research reports on a topic as their information needs evolve (Lacroix and Backus, 2006).

Joint library-information service

It is not just libraries in the traditional sense that may establish joint-use facilities. Increasingly, libraries are combining with one or more information service providers. In the UK many local authorities have now established 'one-stop shops' which provide information about a range of council services; many of these are located in public libraries. Other services that can be found within public libraries include tourist information, children's information, local business information, careers information, citizens' advice, health information and ethnic minority information. The planned joint-use library for the city of Worcester will include a local history centre and the Chamber of Commerce as well as the university, college and public libraries.

Example: Staffordshire Library and Information Service

Staffordshire Library and Information Service has a number of one-stop shops. The first and most successful is in the small market town of Cheadle, UK. Opened in 2001, this came about through the need for both the local district council and the library and information service to relocate their services to more accessible premises. The one-stop facility was established in a shop in the high street, giving all services a much more prominent location in the town, and this brought immediate success with visitor numbers increasing by 195 per cent for library services and 30 per cent for some district council services. One thousand people joined the library in the first five months. The one-stop shop was originally jointly funded by both the county and district councils, with staffing provided by both services; the staff have all since been transferred to the county council to provide single line management and the district council pays towards the staffing costs. The range of services offered from this location has expanded over time and now includes Connexions,[1] pensions services, PCT Pals (Primary Care Trust Patient Advice and Liaison Service), registrars and the CAB (Citizens Advice Bureau). Customer satisfaction with the service is high: 98.5 per cent rate staff helpfulness as very good or good and 94.5 per cent rate the overall service as very good or good. One unexpected spin-off of this development was a reported regeneration in the high street itself, with local businesses reporting an improvement in their activity. The services have expanded to such an extent that larger premises are now required (Jackson, 2007).

Example: Bolton Central Library

In Bolton the Children's Information Service, which was set up in 1999, is managed by the library service and funded by children's services. It is based in the central library. During the day specialist children's information staff answer enquiries and do promotional and outreach work. In the evenings and on Saturdays the central library staff answer the more straightforward questions and take details of more complex enquiries for the Children's Information Service staff to respond to. Parents and carers can access the facility after standard core office hours and obtain a wide range of services, including free internet facilities at the library as well as books for their children. Funding from the Children's Information Service has enabled childcare collections to be set up at all libraries throughout the borough, with information for parents on a wide range of subjects.

Furthermore, the tourist information centre has been based at Bolton Central Library since 2005, but was initially run by separate staff. As part of efficiency savings this service was integrated into the library offer in June 2007 and the tourist information assistants have become library assistants. All central library staff have been trained in answering basic tourism questions, and more detailed enquiries are handled by in-depth library staff who have access to the wide range of information sources online and in stock (Keane, 2007).

Mobile joint-use libraries

Although joint-use libraries are often seen as an alternative to mobile services in rural areas, there are some examples of joint-use mobiles too.

Example: Burton-on-Trent

In Burton-on-Trent, one-stop shops became mobile with the development of a service provided through the Neighbourhood

Management Initiative.[2] This facility was voted for by the local community and provides access to a wide range of services in an area that has a diverse community with many social and economic issues. The mobile has public-access PCs and a private area for information and advice.

Example: Bolton Libraries

In Bolton the library service has attempted to address the decline in the use of mobile services by offering the mobile library along with a library assistant/driver for one day a week as a promotional service for use by other council departments and partner organisations. An additional laptop and 3G internet access for one year were financed by the Neighbourhood Renewal Fund to enable staff to answer enquiries from the public. In 2006–2007 the promotional offer was taken up by a variety of organisations, including Sure Start, the volunteer centre and the council's recycling section.

Other forms of collaboration

Joint-use libraries have been called 'the ultimate form of co-operation' (Bundy, 2003). There are, of course, many other forms of library-to-library collaboration. Just a few examples include:

- resource sharing, for example inter-library loan schemes and the sharing of electronic resources;
- cooperative collection building;
- purchasing consortia;
- joint library and information skills instruction;
- cooperation to encourage reading and literacy;

- contracted services;

- joint projects, e.g. promotion, oral history;

- collections of curriculum materials in public libraries and public library collections in other types of libraries (e.g. the Open University Library houses a small collection of public library adult fiction books and DVDs which can be borrowed using a Milton Keynes Library Service membership card);

- agreements to provide access to limited services, e.g. Libraries Together, Liverpool Learning Partnership[3] and Inspire;[4]

- joint training;

- shared events, e.g. public library/school author visits;

- networking groups.

While such activities *per se* fall outside the scope of this book, they are, of course, important features of joint-use libraries and it has sometimes been the development of a relationship between two or more libraries to carry out these sorts of activities which led ultimately to a joint-use facility being suggested.

Co-location with other services

This book focuses on joint-use facilities developed between two or more libraries or other types of information service. However, it is worth mentioning that there is a growing trend to co-locate libraries, especially public libraries, with other services, such as leisure centres, health centres, banks and other financial institutions, youth centres, childcare facilities, theatres and shops. This is seen as a way to place libraries at the heart of local communities and increase the number of library users, and in particular to target those groups which are traditionally less likely to be library users. Sometimes these facilities offer a range of services targeted at a specific user group, for example young people. While this is undoubtedly an important development and the organisations which work in partnership may well share users, there is likely to be little, if any, overlap in terms of the services and resources offered, potential for shared staffing and so forth, so it is more difficult to consider these co-located facilities as joint-use libraries.

Having discussed what a joint-use library is, the next chapter will consider why this type of library provision is becoming increasingly widespread in the twenty-first century.

Notes

1. Connexions provides advice for 13–19-year-olds on careers, learning, health, legal rights and responsibilities etc.
2. Neighbourhood Management Pathfinders, set up by the Office of the Deputy Prime Minister in 2001, are designed to give residents a real opportunity to improve local services and make them more responsive to their needs. They test a new approach for neighbourhood renewal.
3. See www.liv.ac.uk/library/llgroup/llg.html.
4. See www.inspire.gov.uk/.

2

Why a joint-use library?

Chapter 1 described how joint-use libraries are expanding in number and variety; this chapter will try to explain why this is happening. What factors are stimulating increasing interest in joint-use libraries in the early twenty-first century?

At a theoretical level, there are a number of common catalysts for a joint-use library, including commitment to lifelong learning, initiatives to coordinate cultural institutions, a drive for 'total community library services' and a belief in the rights of citizens to read and have access to information (Karp, 1996). In most cases, however, joint-use libraries are established in response to more practical concerns, such as a requirement to respond to government policy initiatives, pressure for greater economy and efficiency or geographical and demographic factors.

Efficiency and economy

The drive for economy is often a significant factor behind joint-use library proposals. A shared building may well result in reduced overheads for both parties, as heating, lighting, caretaking and similar costs can be shared. Through the sharing of books and other resources, joint-use libraries may also benefit from economies of scale.

Alan Bundy (2007) reports that in South Australia the local government contribution to a joint-use school community library is usually only 2 per cent of property rates revenue, compared with the 6 per cent contribution of rural local councils with stand-alone public libraries. However, joint-use library planners can be naïve about the potential for efficiency savings. In fact, a review of joint-use libraries in the state of Iowa found that per capita expenditure actually increased in the last five communities where school and public libraries combined, partly because school-public combinations were about twice as likely to be ineligible for direct state aid as public libraries in general (State Library of Iowa, 2006).

Some joint-use library proposals suggest there may be reductions in staffing costs, but if a joint-use library is to be an effective resource for all users, this is unrealistic in the majority of cases. It is usually hoped that a joint-use library will result in an increase in user numbers for both libraries, so to provide a level of service which is at least as good as that offered by individual libraries for the increased number and range of users, ample staffing is needed. In fact, in some cases extended opening hours may mean more rather than fewer staff will be needed. ICT is another example of an area where efficiency savings can be overestimated. In many joint-use libraries two networks are needed: a school network with firewalls and a public library network, for instance. In addition, in a joint university-public or college-public library it is likely that additional licences will be required if access to many electronic resources is not to be restricted to academic users.

Example: Blackburn Connected, West Lothian

The business case for this integrated library and customer service centre identified that the benefits would be twofold. Firstly, the prohibitively high maintenance and repair costs associated with the existing library would be eliminated. Secondly, the land could be sold to raise capital of £250,000. The intention was that the council, in partnership with local housing providers, would build low-cost social housing, creating added benefit for the community. Brough (2007) lists some of the cost savings of the centre as a reduction in the cost to the authority for cash collection; an overall reduction in staff numbers; maintenance cost savings of £150,000; and a potential land value of £250,000 through relocating the library.

Policy initiatives

Although more local concerns may dominate in practice, it is certainly the case that government drives promoting collaborative working across library sectors and beyond have favoured the establishment of joint-use libraries in recent years.

However, it is not just recently that policy-makers have encouraged the establishment of joint-use libraries. For more than a century, official reports from education and library agencies have often been catalysts for joint-use provision. In the USA, for example, the *Report of the Committee on the Relations of Public Libraries to Public Schools* (National Education Association, 1899), *School Libraries for Today and Tomorrow* (American Library Association Committee on Post-War Planning, 1945), *Young Adult Services in the Public Library* (Public Library Association Committee on Standards for Work with Young Adults in Public Libraries, 1960) and *Towards a National Program for Library and Information Services: Goals for Action* (National Commission on Libraries and Information Science, 1975) all referred in some way to joint-use provision.

Furthermore, it is not just in the USA that public policy supports the development of joint-use libraries. In Australia, too, political policies and initiatives have supported joint-use provision. In a study in 1978, Dwyer observed that the creation of school-community libraries was consistent with the trend at that time to involve the community in schools and use community facilities for school purposes. In fact, the state of South Australia is the only place in the world to pursue an official plan of rural public library provision through school-housed public libraries. In 1974 the minister responsible for education and the arts decided that the only way to bring a modern public library service rapidly to smaller rural populations was through new federally funded school libraries (Bundy, 1997).

Another example is from Sweden, where the latest amendment to the 1996 Swedish Libraries Act required cooperation:

> County libraries, lending centres, university libraries and university college libraries, research libraries and other libraries funded by the state shall provide literature from their own collections free of charge at the disposal of the public libraries and otherwise co-operate with the public and school libraries and support them in their efforts to offer borrowers good library services. (IFLA, 1996)

In the UK, too, previous policies have encouraged joint-use libraries, although to a lesser extent than those introduced by New Labour since 1997. For instance, a circular issued by the Department of Education and Science in 1970 encouraged local education authorities to seek opportunities to provide facilities in schools which could be shared with the community as a whole. Branch libraries were mentioned as an example of the types of amenities which might be considered, along with welfare agencies and crèches.

Recent UK policy

Perhaps more than anywhere else, recent government policies in the UK have supported the notion of joint-use libraries. Here, the idea of 'joined-up thinking' has dominated at both local and national government levels for the last decade. In 2002 the Audit Commission recommended:

> If the decline in use is to be reversed libraries need to rethink services from the user's point of view [including] improving accessibility by opening at times that suit people, sharing facilities with other services, and using the internet.

One example it gave is of planned improvements to library services in Wilnecote which aimed to relocate from an unsuitable building with poor disabled access to a new arts centre shared with a local high school.

Another significant document in promoting joint-use libraries was 'Empowering the learning community' (Library and Information Commission, 2000). The first recommendation of this report was: 'Public and educational libraries in communities or defined geographic areas should establish co-operative arrangements to improve services to their users.'

However, one of the most recent documents to endorse the idea of partnership working in the public library sector is the Museums, Libraries and Archives Council's 'A blueprint for excellence' (2007). This proposes three key roles for public libraries, one of which is to act as a development agency, joining with partner agencies for targeted interventions to develop the skills and knowledge of individuals, families and communities in learning to read, growing skills, learning for life and supporting disadvantaged and vulnerable groups. Furthermore, nine challenges to improvement are identified, one of which is 'Partnership: working increasingly in partnership – with public, private and third sector partners – to deliver shared outcomes from jointly secured financial and other resources.' Another challenge identified is 'Innovation: exploring new service models and new partnerships better to meet changing customer needs and offer new approaches to service delivery and evaluation.' Joint-use libraries could obviously be an example of such a new approach. A further challenge is improved buildings and access. The blueprint states that up to 70 per cent of community library buildings do not meet the needs of disability access or safety standards; they are dated and deter potential users. Well-designed libraries are 'attractors', both externally and in the configuration and presentation of services. Opening hours and staffing must reflect diverse user needs and contemporary lifestyles. This is precisely what many new joint-use libraries are designed to achieve.

A number of recent policy initiatives have particular significance for joint-use school-public libraries and other facilities with a focus on supporting children and young people. Perhaps the most significant is *Every Child Matters: The Next Steps* (Department for Education and Skills, 2004a). The government published this and passed the Children Act in 2004, providing the legislative spine for developing more effective and accessible services focused around the needs of children, young people and families. Key to this is the idea of multi-agency working and the setting up of Children's Trusts which bring together all services for children and young people in an area.

The development of extended schools is a further driver for the schools sector in the UK. The *Five Year Strategy for Children and Learners* issued by the Department for Education and Skills (2004b) said:

> We want every secondary school to become an extended school, offering:
> - Study support activities
> - Widespread community use of the school's facilities
> - Family learning provided through the school.

All state schools in the UK are now part of an 'extended schools cluster', and by 2010 will provide childcare from 8am to 6pm; a varied menu of activities, including study support; parenting support; referral to specialist support services; and wider community access to ICT, sports, arts and adult learning. The public library service is an obvious partner to support the delivery of a number of these services, and in some cases this has resulted in the establishment of a joint-use library.

In November 2005 the Cabinet Office published *Transformational Government: Enabled by Technology*, which set out the government's vision for a long-term transformation of public services. This affects not just public libraries, but also NHS, school, college and university libraries. One of the three key recommendations was that government should move towards a culture of shared services to improve the quality and cost-effectiveness of public services. Although the concept of shared services is much wider than joint-use libraries, they clearly represent an important element of this vision. In the university sector, the HEFCE (Higher Education Funding Council for England) is establishing an advisory group of experienced senior managers from the sector to assist in taking forward shared services in the sector. The HEFCE (2006) argues 'there are real opportunities for the sector to benefit from adopting shared services, and would encourage HEIs to engage positively with these developments'. Similarly, the Scottish Funding Council has been charged with securing 'efficiency gains through collaboration between institutions, shared support services and new approaches to estates management and development' (Scottish Executive, 2004).

Also in Scotland, the Scottish Executive's (2003a) *Lifelong Learning Strategy* highlights a key role for tertiary education institutions in widening participation and promoting social inclusion. The Scottish government's 'efficient government' initiative and associated reform agenda encourage a 'one-stop shop' approach to public services (Scottish Executive, 2007).

Other government policies and directives have had an indirect effect on decisions to establish joint-use libraries. For example, the 2004 Comprehensive Spending Review led to tighter budgets, combined with the need to make efficiency savings in light of the Gershon Report.[1]

Local policies, too, have had an impact. In Bolton, for example, the council's Change Programme was launched in July 2005 and has four key themes (Bolton Council, 2006b).

- *Customer access*. Making better use of physical points of access to council facilities and encouraging people to use different ways to access council services, such as by the internet and telephone as well as face to face.

- *Seamless services*. Having 'joined-up' services that are centred on customers' needs.

- *Local delivery*. Tailoring services to meet needs of specific communities.

- *Shared services and resources*. Making sure that the council has effective and efficient service delivery.

All of these clearly support the idea of joint-use libraries.

Social concerns

Beyond political and economic concerns, the vast majority of those in the library profession are concerned about social justice and the need to promote community cohesion. The American Library Association (2000) lists 12 ways in which public libraries can build a good community: by informing citizens, breaking down boundaries, levelling the playing field, valuing the individual, nourishing creativity, opening kids' minds, returning high dividends, building communities, making families friendlier, offending everyone (*sic*) offering sanctuary and preserving the past. Many of these can be supported by the formation of a joint-use library. For example, a joint university-public library can break down barriers between local citizens and students; allow access to high-quality academic resources to all; and open young people's minds to the possibility of a university education.

According to IFLA (2001), public libraries 'have an important role in the development and maintenance of a democratic society by giving the individual access to a wide and varied range of knowledge, ideas and opinions'. The following descriptions of public libraries (Bundy, 2004) illustrate both the importance of their role in promoting community cohesion and the potential to achieve this through collaboration with other services:

- cultural cafés;
- urban regenerators;
- street-corner universities;
- community marketplaces;
- empowerment supermarkets;
- into gas stations.

The culture, ideology and approach to the provision of public services in a region or nation can often act to support the concept of joint-use libraries. Public libraries in Scandinavia can be described as being infused with the values and norms of a social democratic welfare ideology. This means that most libraries are publicly funded, owned and managed because the country has a comparatively large public sector where education, healthcare and many other services are delivered by public institutions. Many librarians in Sweden find the vision of a joint-use library appealing because it suggests a way to strengthen the sector and places libraries at the centre of societal development (Zetterlund and Garden, 2007).

Social inclusion as a concept has been recognised in Europe since at least the 1970s, but has been part of the policy agenda in the UK only since 1997. The UK government's earliest definition of social exclusion was relatively unsophisticated:

> A shorthand term for what can happen when people or areas suffer from a combination of linked problems such as unemployment, poor skills, low incomes, poor housing, high crime, bad health and family breakdown. (Vincent, 2005)

Since the 1970s there have been publications identifying the role that public libraries could play in tackling social exclusion, then often labelled 'disadvantage' or 'deprivation'. From the late 1990s there was a further raft of reports looking at the issue: a number of these point out the importance of collaborative partnership working if public libraries are to have a significant role in tackling social exclusion. One example is Roach and Morrison (1998), who focused on public libraries and ethnic minority communities. Among their recommendations were calls for greater integration and partnership between the public library service and related service providers. In 2002, however, research into the role that libraries, archives and museums could play in neighbourhood renewal and social inclusion found there was limited evidence of the sector's working in 'inter-domain or pan-sectoral collaborative partnerships' (Parker et al., 2002).

The Social Inclusion Executive Advisory Group to the Chartered Institute of Library and Information Professionals (CILIP) reported in 2002, recommending that:

> CILIP should encourage LIS organisations to mainstream services to socially excluded people and promote diversity, recognising that for most this will mean organisation transformation... Help to ensure, both by direct provision and by working in partnership with other relevant agencies, that the support mechanisms are available to those organisations undertaking change – training opportunities, best practice information, networks of support. (CILIP, 2002a)

While public libraries have a clear role in promoting community cohesion and encouraging social inclusion by working with other sectors and agencies, academic libraries too are concerned with similar issues through the push to widen participation in education. This has been a focus for UK universities since 2003 when the government's Department for Education and Skills published the white paper *The Future of Higher Education*, which included a clear commitment to widen participation in higher education and address the large discrepancies in the take-up of higher education opportunities between different social groups. School libraries also have a role to play in social inclusion. The *IFLA/UNESCO School*

Library Manifesto (1999) includes the following statement under 'The mission of the school library':

> School library services must be provided equally to all members of the school community... Access to services and collections should be based on the United Nations Universal Declaration of Human Rights and Freedoms.

The commonality between these aims makes a joint-use facility seem like a rational option which might help both library services to be more inclusive organisations. A joint-use university-public library, for example, can benefit both partner libraries and their users by acting as a showcase for the university and making it seem more accessible to local people, perhaps encouraging those who might not otherwise have considered doing so to take a formal course. The role of joint-use libraries in promoting social cohesion is discussed in greater depth in Chapter 6.

Example: Dr Martin Luther King Jr Library, San José

One of the motives for establishing the joint-use public and university library in San José was to improve the poor relationship that had existed between the university and the city. The existing relationship was perhaps best demonstrated by the fact that the university buildings were built with their rear entrances to the city streets, while the front facades faced inwards. English is the language spoken at home for just 45 per cent of the population of the city of San José; in all, 52 languages are spoken. Although the educational level for the community is higher than average, with 36 per cent having a degree, 18 per cent do not have a high school diploma. Household income also varies widely (Kifer, 2007).

Example: North City Library, Manchester

North City Library, which has won two RIBA architecture awards, replaced two very old buildings that were no longer fit for purpose, were expensive to maintain and did nothing to add to the local environment or neighbourhood. In contrast, North City Library is a building which demonstrates pride in the area. This is important because it is an area which has high levels of deprivation and unemployment; low attainments levels in schools; families for whom English is not the first language; low self-esteem; perceptions that anti-social behaviour and crime levels are high; poor parenting strategies; high numbers of young people not in education, training or employment; and significant numbers of teenage pregnancies (MacInnes and Long, 2007).

Geography

Joint-use libraries have, traditionally, been proposed as an effective form of library provision for isolated rural areas, and are often advocated as a superior alternative to an intermittent mobile service.

In Portugal, for instance, small villages and rural communities often do not have a public library, but all have schools. So joint-use libraries are being adopted in some areas as a means of offering public and school library provision. The municipality and the Ministry of Education jointly hold the responsibility of setting up the library within the school. The Ministry of Education is responsible for financing the acquisition of equipment and collections. The public library and the school library have joint responsibility for the selection of resources, and the public library takes charge of the technical servicing of materials and is responsible for promotional activities, in collaboration with the school.

One example of such a library is the project through the School Library Network Programme to build a school-housed library in Barrancos, a small village in a rural area with a population of 2,500. It has a single school for students from pre-primary to high secondary level. As the school library is the only cultural facility in the village, it makes sense to use it to find a solution that will allow access to resources for all the community. This situation led to the local authority and the School Library Network Programme making a formal agreement for a joint-use library. It is located in a converted gymnasium, and the cost of equipment, materials and electronic resources was shared by the two partners. A significant issue was the need for qualified staff who could not only deal with the library management and tasks such as cataloguing, but also respond to the differing needs of users. The solution adopted was for the municipality to pay for a technical librarian, while the School Libraries Network Programme, through the Ministry of Education, provides a school librarian (Martins, 2007).

Research has found that the concept of joint-use libraries is most likely to succeed in rural areas with a population of about 3,500 people (Bundy, 2003). However, in recent years they have become increasingly common in urban localities too. There are many factors behind this: most notably, increased pressure on library services of all types to place themselves at the heart of their communities and attract non-users. Changes in lifestyle may also play a role: as people lead ever-busier lives, library services have to ensure they are convenient and accessible, and many people appreciate being able to combine a library visit with another activity, whether taking a child to school, paying local taxes or visiting a health professional. And it is worth pointing out that isolation can be as much of a problem in some urban localities as it is in rural areas. A road or the edge of an estate, for instance, can seem like a physical boundary in some people's minds – one which they will only cross with reluctance. This makes the siting of library facilities within urban communities an issue which needs careful consideration. It can provide an argument either for or against the provision of a joint-use facility in different circumstances.

Example: Manchester Libraries

Manchester has recently opened three new joint-use libraries in order to improve the condition of the library stock, much of which was in a poor state of repair and located in the wrong places for local communities. Key principles for new library locations include main artery roads, good transport links, prime locations in district centres and iconic civic spaces (MacInnes and Long, 2007).

Demographics

The fact that two or more libraries share a significant proportion of users may suggest that a joint-use library would offer a sensible means of meeting their needs. The 'People flows' report (Mynott et al., 1998) demonstrated the significant overlap between users of different library services. It found that learners do not see themselves as users of one particular library or type of library, and indicated that library users can no longer be pigeonholed into defined library sectors. The research showed that:

- almost one-third of public library users are either full-time students or lifelong learners;

- over two-thirds of the users of university and college libraries also use other libraries;
- almost one-third of other libraries used by university respondents are public libraries;
- over half of the users of public libraries also use other libraries;
- almost 90 per cent of other libraries used by college respondents are public libraries.

These findings are supported by the 1995 Apt Review, which showed evidence of considerable cross-sectoral use of libraries, in particular higher education and further education students making use of public libraries (Apt Partnership, 1995). In the same year, a report by Book Marketing found that 55 per cent of full-time and part-time students used both academic and public libraries, and a further 20 per cent used public but not academic libraries (cited in Hall and Curry, 2000: 38).

Moving on to more localised demographic concerns, the changing population structure of a locality can make a joint-use library an appropriate option, or alternatively may mean that an established library is no longer viable. For example, in Broward County in Florida there has been significant population growth since the mid-1980s, and this is expected to continue. At the same time, Nova Southeastern University expanded considerably from fewer than 20 graduate students in 1964 to 26,000 students in 2007, making it the largest independent institution of higher education in the south-eastern USA. These two factors meant that a joint-use library was felt to be an appropriate means of serving both communities (MacDougall, 2007).

Professional attitudes

During the 1960s and 1970s much of the literature about joint-use libraries had a negative slant: many librarians were very critical of the idea of joint-use facilities. To give examples of some of the many criticisms, they were believed to be bedevilled by conflict between the two organisations; were often poorly located for a public library branch; led to few real savings; were difficult to promote; and suffered because members of the public were reluctant to use a library in a school (White, 1963). In 1972 the UK School Library Association issued a statement claiming that:

> The coming and going of the public will inevitably conflict with the pupils' use of the library space and the head's control of the premises; and the freedom of the public to browse and borrow is bound to be curtailed.

In Australia, Sara Fenwick's 1966 report on school and children's libraries rejected the formal combination of school and public libraries. She later claimed that cheap library provision usually motivated joint use and that, in the USA, school-housed public libraries were usually neither good public libraries nor good school libraries:

> The conclusion to be drawn from studies was that... there appeared to be no real economy, findings were especially critical of the ability of the school-housed branch to provide the depth and variety of resources needed by the users of public libraries, and the failure of the branch to attract adults, out of school youth and preschool children into a service agency located within the walls and jurisdiction of the agency of formal education. (Fenwick, 1975: 23)

The Australian National Inquiry into Public Libraries in 1976, known as the Horton Report, expressed concern that 'schools are generally not well placed to attempt to provide joint school and public library services' (Committee of Inquiry into Public Libraries, 1976: 31).

In more recent years, however, there has been evidence of a change in attitudes and many library professionals have become more positive about the potential of joint-use libraries. This is perhaps no better demonstrated than in the gathering of more than 100 library professionals from around the world in the UK for the first international joint-use libraries conference in 2007. The UK School Library Association, for example, now has a much more encouraging attitude towards joint-use libraries.[2] Literature published since the 1980s, while not overwhelming positive, does highlight many benefits of joint-use libraries. Bundy (2003) and McNicol (2003) have argued that joint-use libraries can promote community interaction and act as a community focal point, increasing understanding between various groups. In the same article, Bundy also claims that joint-use libraries situated in schools or other educational establishments can promote lifelong learning, as these libraries often open for longer hours than their single-sector counterparts, thus improving access. Fitzgibbons (2000) and Bundy (1997) both found that joint-use libraries can offer opportunities for a whole community approach to information literacy development. Furthermore, Stone (1979) and Aaron (1980) reported that joint-use libraries can represent efficient use of public money. Finally, Woolard (1980) said that joint-use libraries can offer a better selection of resources to both user groups.

Organisational goals

If it is to be successful, the creation of a joint-use library will need to fit with the wider goals of all the organisations involved, whether these are pushes to reach new user groups, improve access, make more efficient use of public monies or contribute to community cohesion. The following are just a few examples of how a joint-use library maps on to the organisational goals of the partners involved.

Part of the mission of the Metropolitan State University in Minnesota, USA, is an 'unwavering commitment to civic engagement'. Since its creation in 1971 the university had chosen to utilise existing facilities within the community rather than establish its own library buildings. However, by the 1990s it had grown to such an extent that a library was deemed necessary. Given the university's ethos it is not surprising that it decided to create a library which would not just serve the university, but the local community as well (Barton et al., 2007).

In 2007 Bolton Primary Care Trust (PCT) Learning and Resource Library relocated to a new location within Bolton Central Library. This move was felt to support the goals of both organisations and also coincided with the shared vision of Bolton Council. The UK Department of Health is working towards a 'patient-led NHS' and, as such, there is a need for the general public to make informed choices about their health and lifestyle. Increasingly, the public are also being asked for their opinions and ideas on how NHS services should function. To fulfil these needs there is a requirement for the PCT to provide up-to-date, relevant, easily accessible health information for its communities. One of the PCT's main roles is to improve the health of its population and address health inequalities, and to do this it places a big emphasis on the learning needs of its staff to ensure the delivery of quality services. The provision of an efficient health library service for PCT staff, easily accessible and with opening times outside office hours, is seen as an essential prerequisite. From the public library's perspective, against a backdrop of health impact measures, public libraries are now seen as community resources which can be used in partnership to tackle health inequalities. Furthermore, both the PCT and Bolton Council are working jointly towards achieving the aims of the Bolton vision to help more people to make more informed choices abut their health (Hardman and Melmoth, 2007).

Institutional structures

Although in most cases the decision to opt for a joint-use library is one which is carefully considered and debated, a few such libraries exist simply because of the nature of their parent organisations. This can become quite complicated. For example, in 1989 what were then the Darwin Institute of Technology and University College of the Northern Territory (NT) in Australia merged, to form the Northern Territory University. In 2003 Centralian College in Alice Springs, NT Rural College in Katherine and the Menzies School of Health Research joined with the Northern Territory University to become Charles Darwin University. Hence the library is tripartite, serving university, technical and further education (TAFE) and secondary students. Although the secondary school reverted to being a separate entity in 2005, the library retained its joint-use role (Sumner and Mamtora, 2007). Another example is Thames Valley University in the UK. In 2004 this merged with Reading College and School of Art and Design, thus creating a new educational facility for both higher education and further education students. The library services provided had to adapt to meet the needs of the new student groups, meaning that the library displays many of the characteristics of a joint-use facility although it is not officially recognised as one.

Personalities

It is important not to overlook the importance of personal values and links between partners in decisions to establish joint-use libraries. For instance, in Broward County in Florida there were strong connections between key players in the university and public libraries prior to the establishment of the joint-use Alvin Sherman Library. Nova Southeastern University president Ray Ferrero Jr is a prominent attorney and past president of the Florida Bar Association. He has had strong connections in Broward County for over 40 years. The vice president for administration at Nova Southeastern University, George L. Hanbury II, had previous ties to Broward County as the former city manager of Fort Lauderdale. Sam Morrison, formerly director of Broward County Library, and Donald E. Riggs, vice president for information services and university librarian at Nova Southeastern University, had previous professional ties. All these connections helped during the negotiation and planning stages for the new library (MacDougall, 2007).

According to Kifer (2007), the idea for the Dr Martin Luther King Jr joint-use library in San José originated when the university president and city mayor met informally. The senior positions held by these individuals are crucial. As Jane Light, the director of the public library in San José, has said: 'If this had been an idea of the two library directors, we would still be trying to sell it, above and below. It took bolder leadership at the very top, where the people who control the resources are' (quoted in Kifer, 2007).

Similarly, in Bolton in the UK the creation of a joint-use library facility between Bolton Public Library Service and Bolton PCT, described above, was facilitated by the fact that the director of public health has a post that is jointly funded by both the PCT and the council. The director of public health sits within the management team of the PCT and within Adult Services for Bolton Council. Her work is closely aligned with that of the director of Adult Services. Crucially, both directors embraced the new joint-use library venture from its inception through to its implementation.

Conclusions

It is clear there can be many reasons why a joint-use library might be established; there is usually more than one driver and the combination of factors is unique to each library. The changing attitude towards joint-use libraries within the library profession is, perhaps, one of the most interesting factors. In the past there was a reluctance to 'dilute' library provision by establishing joint-use facilities. Although attitudes are now changing, it is still the case that many joint-use libraries are established in reaction to external events, such as government policy, efficiency drives or organisational changes. In the future, librarians from all sectors will need to be more proactive in the development of joint-use libraries, identifying opportunities where they can provide better services to users through a joint-use facility than via existing facilities. Some librarians and library services have begun to do this, but for others joint-use libraries are still seen as an inferior alternative to a single-sector library.

There is still some way to go before joint-use libraries are embraced throughout the profession as positive developments which, in the right circumstances, can provide superior resources, services, facilities and access to users as well as attracting new users to libraries.

Notes

1. The Gershon Report of 2004 (available at www.hm-treasury .gov.uk/media/C/A/efficiency_review120704.pdf) set out proposals for efficiencies in public spending, identifying annual savings valued at approximately £21.5 billion a year by 2007–2008.
2. See www.sla.org.uk/pol-dual-use-libraries.php.

3

Joint-use library design

Having discussed what a joint-use library is and why it might be established, this chapter asks what does a joint-use library look like? Unsurprisingly, the answers to that question are as varied as the types of, and arrangements for, the libraries themselves. A joint-use library can be a new build on a new site; a new build on or close to the site of an existing library; a conversion of one or more existing libraries; or a conversion of another building or room. Obviously a new build on a new site offers greatest flexibility in terms of location and design, but in practice the design of many joint-use libraries is limited by historical decisions, and compromises usually have to be made for cost reasons too. Trying to cater for the needs of all user groups in the design of a joint-use library is a tricky balancing act, and where a library shares a building with other types of service, the design issues are likely to be even more complex.

At a workshop on this topic at the 2007 international conference on joint-use libraries, it was argued that many of the important design considerations for these libraries would apply to most single-sector library services too – for example, a welcoming entrance, the ability to make flexible use of space, natural light, the adoption of retail innovation and sufficient space for backroom work. However, there are also a number of distinctive design features which are important considerations shared by most, if not all, joint-use libraries.

The guidelines for development of a public library set out by UNESCO and IFLA (2001) list a series of facilities that need to be included in any moderately sized library. They state that:

> In planning a new library the following should be considered for inclusion:
>
> - the library collection including books, periodicals, special collections, sound recordings, and video cassettes and other non-print and digital resources
> - reader seating space for adults, children, and young adults to use for leisure reading, serious study group work, and one-to-one tutoring; quiet rooms should be provided
> - outreach services: spaces should be provided to house special collections and preparation areas for outreach services
> - staff facilities including workspace (including desks or PC workstations), rest space for eating and relaxing during breaks and meeting rooms where staff can meet with colleagues and supervisors in private
> - meeting room space for large and small community groups which should have separate access to the washrooms and the exterior to enable meetings to be held while the library is closed
> - technology including public access workstations, printers, CD-ROM stations, copiers, microfilm/fiche readers, public typewriters, and facilities for listening to recorded sound
> - special equipment including atlas cases, newspaper racks, self-service book circulation, dictionaries,

wall-mounted display racks, display stands, filing cabinets, map cases etc.

- sufficient space for ease of circulation by both public and staff; this can be 15–20 per cent of public areas and 20–25 per cent of staff areas

- in larger libraries a café area for the public is a desirable facility

- space must be allowed for the mechanical services of the library e.g. elevators, heating, ventilation, maintenance, storage of cleaning materials etc.

In his book on public library buildings, Michael Dewe (2006) highlighted the following design factors for joint-use libraries:

- site location: good visibility from and proximity to a major public thoroughfare and adjacent parking;

- access and entry: a common entrance and the public should not have a complicated route to the library;

- external lighting and signposting;

- internal design and furnishing taking into account different age groups using the library etc.

Location

The siting of a joint-use library is, of course, a key consideration. Any library should be located in a position where it can best serve its user community. In the case of joint-use libraries, naturally, this means that the library needs to be located in a position where it can serve multiple user groups. Traditionally, this has been one of the problems faced by school-public libraries. If a school-public library is located within school grounds or, as is often the case, actually in the school itself, this can make it less accessible to the local community. Many people, especially older members of the community or those who do not have pleasant memories of school, may find visiting a library within a school something of an ordeal. Furthermore, often schools, especially secondary schools, are not located in the heart of the local community and close to other services such as shops and healthcare and leisure facilities. So while their location might be ideal for a library serving the school, they do not meet the needs of public library users. The same might be argued to be true of some joint university-public or college-public libraries, especially if the university or college is a campus site located some distance from the nearest residential area.

If an appropriate location can be found which is accessible to all potential users, as Dewe (2006) points out, the precise position of the library on the site is an important consideration. It needs to be visible to, and convenient for, all users. So a joint university-public library, for instance, should be close to the main teaching areas (or halls of residence) for students, while also being visible from the road if possible, and certainly close to the main entrance and parking areas for members of the public. The issue of parking provision at joint-use libraries often leads to heated debate within the local community, and this is discussed further in Chapter 4.

Access and entry

A common entry point for all users is frequently cited as a requirement for a successful joint-use library. However, while this is undoubtedly a benefit for library staff in keeping track of users entering and exiting the library, for a school-public or college-public library in particular there may be arguments in favour of dual entry points.

Security in schools has increased in recent years, and it is now common practice for all visitors to be asked to sign in and display a visitor's pass. However, this can cause problems in joint-use libraries, as such bureaucratic procedures can act as a deterrent to precisely the types of users which public libraries are working to recruit – those who have traditionally not made great use of libraries. The understandable concern for the security of pupils can be at odds with the open, inclusive ethos of public libraries.

Depending on the precise location of the library, it may be appropriate to have an external entry point for public users and another entrance for pupils to access the library directly from the school, but not allowing access back into the school without a security code or pass. This would allow members of the public to use the library, where there is constant staff supervision to ensure children's safety, without having to go through security procedures to gain entry to the school.

If the library is located within the school this is obviously not possible, and public library users will not only have to sign in to use the library but may also have to negotiate a complicated route in order to find it. This problem can be true of other types of joint-use library; for example, many university libraries now also require visitors to display some form of identification. Ensuring that joint libraries are open and accessible to all is a concern for public libraries in particular, and is an issue which needs careful consideration when planning a joint-use library.

External signposting

Good external signage is crucial to attract library users. Joint-use libraries need to remember that their users may be approaching the library from different directions. In a school-public library, for example, public users will approach from the road, while pupils will come to the library from other parts of the school. Signs need to make it clear who the library is for. The name of the library can be a tricky issue. Having the title 'school-community library' might appear to some to indicate a library for the school community; members of the public need to be aware that the library is not just for the school community, but also for the local community. Another complication is that many school, college and university libraries are renaming themselves as learning resource centres. While this title may be understood by students and teachers, members of the public are less likely to recognise this as a library.

Sometimes the library building itself can be thought of as acting as a form of signage. An impressive, well-sited building which is visible for a distance can point out the location of the library far better than any traditional signage. The way in which the library is lit at night can also act as a means of directing people to the building. An obvious practical point is that the approach to the library should be well lit and feel safe at night as well as during the day.

Internal design and furnishing

There are a number of important considerations in the internal design of a joint-use library. While many will also apply to other types of library, the issues discussed in this section are particularly crucial in ensuring the success of a joint-use facility.

Space and layout

The amount of space available in a joint-use library is often not ideal, especially if the library originally served a single user group and has been converted into a joint-use facility. Many staff working in joint-use libraries say it is important not to underestimate the amount of space which will be needed. However, some new libraries are being built that scarcely accommodate existing use, never mind possible future expansion if the library is successful in generating extra use, the local population increases or the library is required to offer new services.

But how large does a joint-use library need to be? One difficulty facing joint-use library planners is that standards and guidelines for size only usually refer to a single library sector – for example, IFLA's (2001) guidelines for public libraries. IFLA acknowledges that there is no universal consensus on the space required for a public library: 'The amount of floor-space required by a public library depends on the unique needs of the individual community as determined through a community needs assessment and the level of resources available.' Based on standards developed in the USA and Canada, it recommends:

- For a community under 100,000 population the appropriate standard is 56 sq. m. (600 sq. ft.) per 1,000 capita.

- Collection space can be determined by using the average standard of 110 volumes per sq. m. (10.8 sq. ft.).

- A generally accepted standard for user space in a library is 5 user spaces per 1,000 capita.

- A space of 2.8 sq. m. (30 sq. ft.) for each reader station is an acceptable standard.

- A public Internet station may be provided at one station per 5,000 population.

- Staff space can be determined by using a total space per staff member of 16.3 sq. m. (175 sq. ft.).

- 20 per cent of net space is also required for building services including washrooms, space for caretakers and cleaners, storage for cleaning materials, mechanical services (heating, ventilation, air-conditioning), elevators, staircases, etc.

- The minimum size for an independent library should not be less than 350 sq. m. (3,770 sq. ft.). In a multi-branch system, the branch should have not less than 230 sq. m. (2,500 sq. ft.) of floor space plus 14 sq. m. (150 sq. ft.) for each additional 1,000 volumes over 3,000 volumes in its collection.

However, this only deals with the public library element. Other partner organisations may have their own recommended size guidelines, but how these are combined where space is shared is not clear. In addition, guidelines do not exist for all sectors or types of services provided in joint-use facilities; in many joint-use combinations, one or more of the partner organisations may not have any guidelines to refer to.

Of course, given the diversity of joint-use libraries, developing standards for every possible combination is unrealistic. However, there are some guidelines for the most prevalent and established types of joint use. Queensland Government's (2005) joint-use public/school library standards state that the joint-use facility should be at least the sum of the floor areas of the separate facilities, less any duplicated facilities. Its recommendations for floor space are less than the IFLA guidelines for public libraries (Table 3.1).

Table 3.1 Recommendations for floor space in joint-use libraries

Population	Area size (m²)
Up to 15,000	42–38 m² per 1,000 population
15,000–50,000	40–36 m² per 1,000 population
50,000+	38–34 m² per 1,000 population

Source: Queensland Government (2005).

However, it must be remembered that the users of a joint-use library are likely to access the library for a more diverse range of purposes than would be the case for a single user group. For example, students will require study space, classes will require teaching space, young children require space for story times and craft activities, reading groups need meeting space, and so forth.

The increasing importance of technology has altered the space which all types of libraries allocate to different activities, but this is likely to be a particular concern in joint-use libraries where there might be a need to have computers connected to different networks. In addition, in a joint academic-public library computers may have to be made available for longer time periods than would be the case in a public library, because students need to use PCs to complete assignments and similar activities. The management of technological resources is discussed in greater detail in Chapter 4.

As well as the amount of space available, the way in which the library is laid out needs careful consideration. It is important that all potential users feel they have an equal entitlement to use the library and that their needs are adequately catered for. A joint-use library is likely to be a more diverse environment than that found in most other types of library; a greater variety of activities have to be encompassed within the library. This means that ways have to be found to mark off certain areas for group work, quiet study, events, computer use and so on, and to indicate the purpose of these areas to users.

A further point is that the layout of a joint-use library needs to allow flexibility, as the composition of the user groups may change over time and adjustments may have to be made. This is also true of use on a day-to-day basis. The provision to convert formal learning spaces for classes into less formal areas which can be used by reading groups, for example, might be a valuable feature of a joint school-public or college-public library.

Entrance

It is vital that the entrance to the joint-use library is welcoming to all potential users; it needs to encourage all types and ages of user to enter the library. As well as features such as signage, it is important to consider the types of resources and services which are visible to users as they enter. Public library users greeted by shelves of academic textbooks may not feel the library is intended for them, for example. Staff presence at or near the entrance can be a way to welcome users and help to guide people to the types of resources and services they are looking for.

Signage is critical in a joint-use library, both at the entrance and elsewhere, to guide users through to the areas of the library they wish to use. This is especially true of larger libraries, such as university-public libraries and those occupying multiple floors.

Interior design

Colour schemes can be used to denote different areas of a library, indicating the purpose it is intended for and the level of noise expected. This is a method which can be, and has been, used successfully in many types of library, but would seem to be especially suited to joint-use facilities where there is perhaps greater need than elsewhere to indicate zones devoted to different activities. Sound or music may be another way to indicate the different zones of a library.

The furnishing of a joint-use library can present challenges because of the need to appeal to different groups. However, this can be linked to zoning and colour schemes to ensure that the environment in each zone of the library is appropriate for the majority of users of that area. Although an overall consistent theme needs to be preserved throughout, there is no reason why different areas cannot have their own unique design features.

Taking account of users in library design

Community engagement is dealt with in greater depth in Chapter 6. However, it is important to remember that engagement with user communities, and also library staff, should begin at the earliest stages of planning a joint-use library. It is not just the library services involved who will need to consult with users: architects meet with user groups during the design phase to present ideas and get feedback, often using 3D sketches, models and fly-throughs. In the UK this process is now more formalised than in the past; the DQI (Design Quality Indicators)[1] questionnaire looks at functionality (use, access and space), build quality and the impact of the building on the local community and environment.

Case study: reconfiguring library space to cater for different user needs at Alice Springs Campus of Charles Darwin University

According to Sumner and Mamtora (2007), the biggest challenge of this joint-use library is trying to provide a service to three vastly different client groups without one group being more demanding of services to the detriment of the others. Undoubtedly, school pupils tend to dominate group study areas where they are able to work together on assignments and discuss ideas and issues – and, inevitably, these discussions tend to get quite heated at times and noise levels rise accordingly. On the other hand, many of the VET (vocational education and training) and HE (higher education) students are mature students and prefer a quiet space where they can work in peace and are able to concentrate on what they are doing. In a small, open-plan library it has been difficult to provide the study spaces that these distinctive client groups require. The library attempted to compensate by sectioning off a small area and converting it into a designated quiet study area for VET/HE students. There are 18 computers in this area as well as study desks and a small lounge area for those students who prefer a more relaxed way of working. In 2004 the library was rearranged in an attempt to divide up the space into an interactive, noise-tolerant study space for one group, and a quiet study space using the shelves of the main collection to divide up the areas for the other group (Figure 3.1). While this has produced some benefits, it has not been a complete success as noise still travels into the quiet area.

Case study: concern for practical user needs and striking design features at the Alvin Sherman Library, Florida

Harriet MacDougall (2007) has described how, during the design and planning of the Alvin Sherman Library, much

Figure 3.1 The Charles Darwin University Library, Alice Springs Campus, looking from the noise-tolerant area to the quiet study area

thought was given to how the community would use the library. The planners wanted to create a comfortable space for community members to gather. This resulted in a café being added so that students and public users could have the convenience of a meal during their library visit. The idea was that with an easy meal, library patrons could stay longer and be more comfortable in the setting. The café also provides an informal gathering space with coffee and food for poetry readings, small group meetings and book-club meetings. To help young parents, two drive-by book drops were added. This allows a care-giver to remain in the car with infants and toddlers while returning books and other library materials.

Integrated into the design of the building was a plan to contain noise and preserve quiet areas in the busy library. The library has a stunning atrium that is glassed off on the third, fourth and fifth floors, thus maintaining an area for quiet study. Twenty-two study rooms provide further quiet areas for groups.

Artwork in the library is central to the design, not an afterthought, and is a feature which brings in members of the community. Recently a dramatic Dale Chihuly glass sculpture was permanently installed. This is 17 feet (five metres) long and set on black granite to accentuate its dramatic interplay of colours (Figure 3.2). It is the only Chihuly glass sculpture available for view by the public for free in the area. Following a visit by the Dalai Lama, a Tibetan prayer wheel was created for the library; this permanent installation is one of the largest prayer wheels of its type.

Case study: Oak Park Joint-use Library, California

Jointly developed by the county of Ventura in California and the Oak Park Unified School District, this library (Figure 3.3) serves Oak Park High School students and the surrounding community. The library opened in 2004 and has been awarded a Savings by Design award for energy efficiency. Eco-friendly features include windows in the children's room, study room and main support areas which frame views to an adjacent park, and a courtyard with a specimen oak creating a shaded area for public functions. The programme required an environmentally sound, energy-efficient design and the demonstration of related economic benefits in order to secure a grant from the local air pollution control district. Sustainability goals that are addressed include landscape restoration, water-use efficiency, energy efficiency, air pollution reduction and maximising daylight and views. Interior wall finishes are exposed CMUs (concrete masonry units), which maximises available thermal mass to the interior and minimises painted surfaces. The mass properties of masonry are used to

Figure 3.2 The Dale Chihuly glass sculpture, Alvin Sherman
Library

modulate temperature. Floor finishes include recycled-
content carpet, cork, linoleum, ceramic tiles and exposed
concrete. Ceilings are recycled-content acoustic tiles and
gypsum board, or exposed to structure. Daylight-saving

Figure 3.3   Oak Park Joint-use Library, California

Architect: Harley Ellis Devereaux; sustainable design consultant/specialist: GreenWorks Studio.

goals are achieved through high utilisation of natural light, reflected light and diffused daylight, skylight wells and photocell-controlled light fixtures.

Virtual design

It is not just the design of the library building which needs to be considered; the webpages of a joint-use library also need careful planning. At present this is often neglected, as many joint-use libraries simply adopt the style of one or more of the main partners. However, with the increasing importance of an effective web presence and links to online resources, this is something which will need to be given greater consideration in the future.

A promising model is the Alvin Sherman Library in Florida, which has developed not just two but seven 'patron portals'. As the overview explains:

> The population of patrons we serve is quite diverse, which contributes to the uniqueness of the Alvin Sherman Library. Because we strive to provide the best possible service to all of our users, we have compiled a set of customized site maps, or patron portals, for each of these user groups. (Alvin Sherman Library, Research, and Information Technology Center, 2006).

Thus local students, distance students, alumni, faculty and staff, children, teenagers, adults and seniors citizens each have a dedicated entry point to the library. Naturally, some components are common to all groups, such as how to obtain a library card, but each portal highlights the resources and services which are most likely to be of interest to a particular group of users. Similarly, the Dr Martin Luther King Jr Library in San José offers seven 'paths to lifelong learning', including a portal for the business community. It is also notable that the KidsPlace and TeenWeb portals have a different look and feel to the adult pathways (SJLibrary.org, 2007b).

Conclusions

Designing a joint-use library is certainly not an easy task. Unlike other types of libraries, there are no standard guidelines or models to follow. In the case of school-public libraries there are more established examples to investigate and evaluate in order to decide what is likely to work; but for newer forms of joint-use library there are few long-standing examples. The scale of projects such as the creation of a new university-public library and the shortage of comparable facilities make the process a risky one for designers, architects, funders and the library services involved. However, it is important that these risks are taken in the hope of discovering better models of library provision for the future. As more lessons can be learnt from facilities which have recently been developed, the risks will be reduced.

It is essential that the needs of users and library staff remain central to the planning process. Whatever design is chosen, a joint-use library needs to work effectively for its users and staff. Perhaps above all, a joint-use library should be designed in a way which will appeal to all its potential user groups. It should not look like a school or college library, a university library or even a public library. The designers of joint-use libraries require the vision to create something different from the standard models. As has been described in this chapter, the Alvin Sherman Library in Florida makes use of artworks and other design elements to help forge its unique identity. Similarly, The Bridge in Glasgow defines its distinctive character with its open feel, high ceilings, use of lighting and large expanses of glass. This has created an environment which does not feel as though it is solely the province of either students or the public, but is a resource which is open to all.

Note

1. See www.dqi.org.uk/dqi.

4

How does a joint-use library operate?

The last chapter considered what a joint-use library looks like. But how does it function? How is it managed? And how does it operate on a day-to-day basis? Just as a joint-use library differs from other types of library in certain aspects of its design, it also requires new operational procedures to be developed. Librarians in different sectors have traditionally adopted their own working practices, and these will need to be reconciled in a joint-use facility. This chapter examines issues such as management, governance, staffing, collection development and other operational matters. It starts, however, with what could be seen as the most important factor: the service-level agreement, or memorandum of understanding.

The agreement

Over a number of years the literature has identified the key success factors for joint-use libraries. One of these is the need for a formal agreement endorsed by all cooperating authorities. The agreement should include the essential items but not attempt to cover all policy issues. The main key areas which need to be emphasised are space, staffing and staff development, information technology, the role of the governing body and evaluation. The agreement should also provide for dissolution of the joint-use library.

Many joint-use libraries, especially those which have opened more recently, have realised the importance of a service-level agreement. Writing about The Bridge in Glasgow, Cathy Kearney (2007: 137) said:

> The service level agreement is crucial for the smooth delivery of the shared service. Its function is to support the new operation by giving careful attention to ensuring that the needs of college staff and students are met within the new arrangements. The agreement is general and non-prescriptive, affording sufficient latitude to allow local resolution of difficulties. However, it also includes formal processes for problem resolution and for periodic review and revision to take account of changed circumstances.

Gipsyville in Hull is a very different type of joint-use library, but the service-level agreement is equally important, according to Sue Richmond (2007: 68):

> The library service is now managed through a Service Level Agreement (SLA) which sets out the responsibilities of each partner, operation of the service and performance indicators. The SLA is monitored through the Library Management Board.

At the Alvin Sherman Library in Florida an agreement was signed before any detailed planning commenced, two years before the library opened:

> The agreement was signed with full support from the governing bodies of both entities in December 1999. It is

a 54 page, 40 year agreement laying out details such as how many hours the library will be open to the public – 100 hours per week; the funding for building the library and a parking facility – $44 million in costs divided 50-50; the ongoing support of the building and its collections – divided 60% by the University and 40% by the County; the ownership of the building and its materials – by Nova Southeastern University; and the staffing of the library – all are Nova Southeastern University employees. This agreement does not include the other major libraries at Nova Southeastern University – the Law Library, the Health Professions Library, and the Oceanography Library. The details of the agreement fully lay out the parameters of this joint venture. (MacDougall, 2007: 94)

However, there are still joint-use libraries being opened without an agreement in place. For instance, it took more than two years of negotiations to achieve a service agreement for the school-public library in Winnersh, UK. This meant that the concept of what a joint-use community library is about and what the staff and managers should be aiming to achieve was not clear from the start (McNicol, 2003). Candy Hillenbrand (2005) reports that, although the Mount Barker Community Library in South Australia has been operating under the conditions set out in its agreement for five years, the Institute of Technical and Further Education has yet to sign this agreement, meaning that the long-term financial future of the library is not fully secure. At the Alice Springs Campus of Charles Darwin University in Australia there is currently no memorandum of understanding between the university and the secondary school which share the site. This means the relationship between the two can be strained at times, and library staff can find it difficult to juggle priorities with demands coming from both sides (Sumner and Mamtora, 2007).

Governance

Another critical success factor established in previous research is that a governing board should participate in the establishment of the joint-use library, to develop ongoing broad policy for its operation and determine goals and budget priorities. At Rockingham Regional Campus Community Library in Australia, for instance, a policy advisory committee was introduced from the very first to support the campus librarian, with representation from all stakeholder groups. Although this committee met regularly at first, over time the frequency of meetings has reduced as there have been fewer problems to discuss (Hamblin, 2007). At Gipsyville in Hull the library management board meets quarterly, and is composed of the centre manager (PANDA, the Pickering and Newington Development Association), the library and reception manager (PANDA), a senior library manager and representatives from the PANDA management board (Richmond, 2007).

Management

According to the literature on joint-use libraries, the library director should be a professional librarian who has the freedom to manage, including having direct control of staff and budgets. In practice, however, who has overall responsibility for the management of a joint-use library varies from one library to another. Whether there are two or more managers with shared responsibilities or a single library manager would seem to depend, at least in part, in the degree of integration between the library services. Where there are essentially two separate library services sharing a building with separate budgets, staffing and so forth, having two managers would seem a reasonable solution. However, in a truly integrated library a single manager is usually necessary. If there is more than one manager/director, there needs to be a clear agreement setting out what decisions each is responsible for and where one has to defer to the other. In this situation, the governing body is likely to be particularly important in making, or at least endorsing, decisions which will affect the whole library rather than just one of the partners.

Having a single library director is, without doubt, a simpler, more efficient and less ambiguous system of management. However, most library directors are likely to have had a background primarily in a single library sector, and so will need support from deputies with expertise in the other sector(s) involved, especially during their early years in post.

Communication

A number of success factors have been identified relating to the importance of effective communication, both within the joint-use library itself and with external bodies.

- The library director should be represented on the senior decision-making and policy bodies of each constituent institution.
- Direct two-way communication should occur between the director and funding bodies.
- Regular consultation with, and reporting to, all parties concerned should occur.

The methods by which communication between the various stakeholder groups occurs vary from library to library, and each joint-use library needs to find the solution which works for its individual circumstances. The following are just two examples of how committees and groups communicate.

At The Bridge in Glasgow a number of groups help to ensure effective communication and decision-making. Operational decisions are taken in the context of a joint group chaired by John Wheatley College's information and learning services manager. The operational group in turn is supported by weekly informal meetings between college and library staff. A steering group, whose role is to monitor progress, meets quarterly and includes senior representatives from Culture and Sports Glasgow and the college management, as well as advisory input from the JISC (Joint Information Systems Committee) Regional Support Centre Scotland South West and the Scottish Library and Information Council. Finally, the pedagogic link between the service and learning and teaching activities is maintained through senior library service representation on the college academic board (Kearney, 2007).

At the Alvin Sherman Library in Florida, the head of circulation regularly attends the circulation managers' meeting of Broward County Library staff. Here information is exchanged that creates more effective procedures to manage the circulation functions for all patrons. There is a regular meeting for collection development staff, and members from both groups work towards making the best collection choices for the larger clientele. The content of the meetings may vary, but the intent is to foster greater collaboration and work towards making the library a successful venture for both groups (MacDougall, 2007).

Both these are large-scale joint-use libraries. In a smaller joint-use school-public library there are likely to be fewer formal committees and perhaps more informal communication. However, regardless of the size or type of joint-use library, it is imperative that there are clear lines of communication between all partners and library managers. Where the most appropriate person does not attend meetings, problems can develop. Patricia Bauer (2007) describes how, under the new chain of command at West St Petersburg Community Library in Florida, the community-use librarian no longer attends branch library meetings of the city: the head librarian, a college reference librarian, has this role. This effectively diminishes the public library's role in the collaboration.

Budgets

The amount that each partner contributes to the joint-use library, or the types of services and resources they are responsible for providing, obviously needs to be clearly set out from the start. However, this can be a contentious issue and the solutions adopted vary considerably. The examples below illustrate the diversity of practice and the complexity of budgeting in joint-use libraries.

At the joint Daytona Beach Community College/University of Central Florida library the budgets for each institution are separate. The UCF budget comes from the regional campus budget rather than the UCF library budget. There is no set materials budget for the regional campus libraries: the amount received varies from year to year, and in some years there is no money for these libraries. This process is changing and there will gradually be a more constant budget. The DBCC budget is more stable, but the amount received has not changed in several years. This means that fewer materials can be purchased each year as costs rise due to inflation. In addition, materials for the baccalaureate programme come from yet another cost centre (Bozeman and Owens, 2007).

At Rockingham Regional Campus Community Library in Australia, operational funding was initially divided equally between the three partner organisations on the premise that a funding formula would be agreed in the future. Although on the basis of library loans the city might be expected to contribute 86 per cent of operating costs, the university and TAFE users occupy significantly more staff time with the provision of information literacy and reference services. To date, an acceptable level of funding for each group has not been agreed; at present the university contributes 42 per cent, the city 33 per cent and the TAFE sector 25 per cent.

Determining an appropriate level of contribution for each partner in a joint-use library is highly complex. It is not an easy matter to agree a budgeting formula that all partners find acceptable. At Mount Barker Community Library in South Australia there has been a significant delay in signing the service-level agreement because of disagreements over funding levels. While only 5.6 per cent of the library users are TAFE staff or students, the college provides 18 per cent of the budget in addition to financing the upkeep of the building, and it was unwilling to commit to this level of funding (Hillenbrand, 2005).

It is not as simple as looking at loan figures, because different user groups will use the service in different ways and make more, or less, use of different types of resources and services. As Deb Hamblin (2007) points out, little work has been done on the cost of providing library services to public members compared to education users, and the same is true of knowledge about the relative costs of providing services for other user groups. She makes another interesting point about the need for funding formulas to be flexible to meet the changing demands of user groups. She explains that although traditionally TAFE students have not been heavy library users, hence the smaller contribution of the sector to the overall budget, this is changing. Although the TAFE contribution needs to be increased to reflect this, to base the level solely on percentage use would not be an acceptable solution; rather, costs have to be compared to those at other TAFE libraries.

Staffing

Staffing is probably the most complex operational issue facing most joint-use libraries. The role of staff in these libraries is very different from that of staff serving a single user group. The staff composition and structure must respond to the needs of the whole user community of the library.

The success factors relating to staffing in joint-use libraries include:

- staffing levels should be adequate, and the composition of the staff should reflect the requirements of the profile community;
- staffing should be integrated it possible;
- support structures should discourage too rapid fluctuations in staffing numbers.

The skills required by staff working in joint-use libraries should not be underestimated. As Deb Hamblin (2007: 74) says:

> we need to be incredibly multi skilled. Being a remote campus the library provides everything from student cards to IT assistance for wireless and help with printing, copying and scanning. There is no such luxury as subject specialization and we help nurses, engineers and

historians as well as electricians and bricklayers. We then of course have to be entertaining enough to offer school holiday activities and regular story telling sessions.

However, it is not just the range of skills required which means that work in a joint-use library is not a suitable career move for all members of the profession. As Zetterlund and Garden (2007) point out, 'the vision of joint use libraries often includes crossing professional boundaries', and this can be problematic, especially if some staff are reluctant to expand their professional horizons. This might be because of fears about loss of status. When the idea of establishing a joint-use university-public library in San José was first mooted, the response was far from positive. In fact university librarians, along with faculty members, formed a group called SOUL (Save Our University Library). The university librarians created a document entitled 'Affirming academic responsibilities' which enumerated the values and responsibilities of academic librarians, principally to support teaching, learning and research. Public library staff expressed similar concerns and a corresponding document entitled 'Affirming San José Public Library Service' was also produced (Kifer, 2007).

Traditionally, the majority of library professionals have tended to spend their careers in a single sector. Van House et al. (1983) reported on a study of the library labour market in the USA. This examined a sample of librarians in public, academic, special and school district libraries to discover the future supply and demand for librarians in the profession. The authors found that both employers and librarians create barriers to movement across sectors:

> Although in theory librarians can move around among types of libraries, in practice they generally don't. This

may be because librarians prefer to stay with one type of library. Or it may be that the labour market is actually several markets with permeable boundaries. Employers (and librarians) may perceive that librarians' skills are not transferable across library types. (Van House et al., 1983: 364)

Koenig and Safford (1984) explored reasons for a shortage of competent managerial-level staff in academic research libraries in the USA. They suggested that within the profession, and particularly the academic research library sector, there is a problem of 'vertical stratification' where different sectors of the profession perceive themselves as being separate. They commented:

We act as if public librarianship were almost a different career from, for example, academic librarianship. There are differences, of course, but hardly the sort that should prevent individuals from moving from one venue to another. (Koenig and Safford, 1984: 1899)

They refer to a 'type of library mythology' whereby librarians believe that different sectors 'are distinct career paths to which one must make a commitment early in one's career'.

Dalton et al. (1999) reported the following institutional and individual barriers to crossing sectors:

- Employers express a preference for sectoral experience and fail to acknowledge the transferability of skills
- Jobs are not advertised outside the sector
- Job advertisements do not encourage applicants from outside the sector

- LIS professionals moving to a new sector may require more training than individuals already familiar with a sector
- Lack of confidence in, and awareness of, the transferability of skills between different sectors of the profession
- Use of specialist recruitment agencies.

Staff in joint-use libraries need to be committed to, and enthusiastic about, the concept of joint use. Those who are accustomed to a certain way of working or type of user may not immediately see the benefits of a joint-use facility. When new staff are to be recruited, there is more flexibility and the level of commitment to the concept of a joint-use library can be explored at interviews. However, in many instances the majority of staff in a new joint-use library will be those who were previously employed in one or other of the stand-alone libraries involved in the partnership. To convince staff of the potential benefits, it is important that they are involved in the development of the joint-use library from the early planning stages. In the Blackburn Connected project in Scotland, for instance, the team were informed about the initiative and given the option of joining the new team or being redeployed. The team themselves worked on writing new job descriptions, performance indicators and a community engagement programme (Brough, 2007). Similarly, some library staff at Platt Bridge Community First in Wigan, UK, expressed initial concern about the changes, so the project manager tried to keep them informed and involved in the process through site visits, newsletters and other means, and most came to appreciate the benefits. Working with staff from other services was tricky at first, but this has become easier as people from different backgrounds have come to know each other and develop working relationships (Evidence Base, 2007). At Worcester in the UK, where a new library and history centre is being planned for 2011, staff consultation has been a feature of the planning process right from the start, including focus groups to discuss initial ideas of what might go on in the building and how the different services might work together; staff visits and shadowing, enabling staff from different services to get a feel for how their colleagues work and how they might work together; and small groups of staff working on detailed plans (Fairman, 2007).

A joint-use library may well require additional staff. The creation of the Alvin Sherman joint-use library in Florida, for example, led to the size of the staff more than doubling to cope with a larger building and longer opening hours. In particular, there was a need for more staff where there was most contact with users – for example in circulation and reference services. In addition, specialist youth service librarians were hired to create programmes and services for younger users. It is interesting that when reference staff were hired, preference was given to those with a mixture of public and academic experience. However, it was found that very few librarians have had training or experience in working with such varied user groups. Quinlan and Tuñón (2005: 117) reported that library school training which prepares students for work in a single sector has made it a challenge to recruit and retain staff. In particular, 'some academic librarians do not like the idea of working with the public and would have preferred to let the public libraries deal with "problem" patrons'.

Differences in terms and conditions for librarians working in different sectors can be brought to a head by the creation of a joint-use library. If staff working in a joint-use facility are employed on different terms and conditions, this can lead to tension. At Rockingham Regional Campus Community Library in Australia, before the tripartite agreement was formalised the library staff members were employed under two separate industrial awards, working different numbers of hours per week, getting different pay rates and working different public holidays. The impact of these variant awards led to low morale and a very dysfunctional staffing structure. So, before the move to the new building, positions at the joint-use library were offered to all current staff at Murdoch University, Challenger TAFE and the city of Rockingham libraries. Only one substantive staff member decided not to transfer to the joint library. The remainder signed a contract ensuring seamless service to all stakeholder groups. The management team looked at the awards for each group and decided that the university offered the most favourable terms and conditions, so these were adopted for the single staffing structure (Hamblin, 2007).

Similarly, at The Bridge in Glasgow an early decision was taken to migrate to a single library management system – that of Culture and Sport Glasgow. Staff integration was achieved by ensuring that all were employed by a single employer, sharing common service conditions and working hours. College library staff transferred to Culture and Sport Glasgow under TUPE[1] regulations. A collaborative spirit and team approach have been among the defining features of The Bridge's development as staff faced new work roles, a changing client base, new training requirements and a different work environment and culture (Kearney, 2007). The library staff themselves emphasise the importance of working as a single team with everyone providing the same level of service to all users.

Conversely, at the West St Petersburg Community Library in Florida the divisions between staff have presented difficulties. It is true that users are served in the various departments by librarians who are specialists in their field. However, the downside of this is that there is a lack of collaborative spirit among the staff, some of whom are resistant to working with different client groups (Bauer, 2007).

The following description of staffing arrangements at Gipsyville Library in Hull illustrates the challenges of developing a staffing structure for a joint-use library. The staffing structure at Gipsyville consists of:

- the centre manager
- a library and reception manager
- a team of six library and reception assistants: two library staff who are employed by Hull Libraries and have been seconded to PANDA; two reception assistants employed by PANDA; and two assistants employed by PANDA but whose posts are jointly funded.

Professional librarians from Hull Libraries support the service at the multipurpose centre by undertaking staff training, stock work and promotional events. Hull Libraries has a pool of casual relief staff who can be called upon to provide support with cover for staff training or sickness. All the assistants have new job descriptions which reflect the shared tasks and responsibilities. They are expected to undertake all the tasks associated with the library and reception service, and do not operate as separate teams.

Creating this single team was a challenge, as staff were apprehensive about the change. The reception staff were especially concerned about how the library and its management system operated. To allay these fears a training programme was developed. This began with an informal session in which staff were asked to select activities for increasing the usage of the library and multipurpose centre from predetermined action cards, and to identify what training and support they would need to accomplish these selected actions. This training helped to bring the teams together to understand their new roles and discover that not only did they share the same apprehensions but that they could also help each other by sharing knowledge, skills and experience. Further training involved:

- job swaps, with library staff timetabled to work on reception so the reception staff could work in the library;

- working at an area HQ – this is a bigger, busier library, so staff could develop their confidence;

- opening the library on a Tuesday morning staffed by the reception staff – this allowed the staff to implement their new knowledge and skills and proved a real confidence-booster.

Finally, new timetables were introduced to extend the library opening hours from 30 to 50 hours per week. In February 2006 the two teams began operating the new library and reception service (Richmond, 2007).

When speaking informally, many joint-use librarians comment on the positive aspects of working in such a challenging environment. This is often lost in official reports on staffing in joint-use libraries. However, some comments captured in a survey of South Australian joint-use librarians (reported in Bundy, 2007: 117) illustrate the enthusiasm which many joint-use library staff feel for their work:

> A community library is a fantastic place to work in – no two days are ever the same!

> I love the job, but it is hard not to give too much of your own time and resources to projects at times!

But this survey also pointed out that working in a joint-use library is not an easy option! There needs to be adequate support for staff in terms of resources, training and, perhaps most important of all, endorsement and appreciation of their work from those in senior positions in the partner organisations.

Collection development and management

Of course, like any library, a joint-use library needs a collection development policy. However, who is responsible for stock selection and technical processing and how this occurs are often complicated processes in a joint-use library.

In any type of library there are usually specialist staff responsible for the purchase of the various collections. In a public library this might include children's stock, audio-visual materials and reference resources, for example. In an academic library there is division by subject discipline. It is important to maintain the professional expertise which specialists in each of these areas bring to the development of collections, as well as to other library services.

In addition to the question of who is responsible for resource selection, which partner is responsible for providing the various resources that joint-use library users might wish to see in the library needs to be resolved. In a joint-use school-community library, for instance, it is usual for the school to take primary responsibility for the development of a collection to support the curriculum, while the public library focuses its attention on resources to promote wider reading, lifelong learning and meeting the needs of users outside the age group catered for at the school. A similar principle seems to be followed in most other types of joint-use library, with each partner concentrating its resources on the collections it would be most likely to maintain in a stand-alone facility. For example, at the Metropolitan State University St Paul Campus in Minnesota the university develops its library resources to support the curriculum and academic programmes, although it may purchase some items for public library borrowers, especially if these are also likely to be of interest to academic users. The public library, on the other hand, orientates its collection and services towards families, with a special focus on children and young adults (Barton et al., 2007).

At Daytona Beach Community College/University of Central Florida joint-use library in the USA, each library purchases materials for the joint-use library from separate budgets. Each institution has its own acquisitions and technical services department. The process that produces the joint-use collection is time-consuming and disjointed. When selecting items for purchase, the UCF and DBCC librarians work together to choose materials that will support the programmes offered by both institutions at the Daytona campus, and to avoid duplication. Librarians work with their respective faculty to ensure that all classes are supported and faculty have the materials needed. Before ordering, librarians must check both catalogues for duplicate titles.

All technical services functions are carried out centrally at the main campus libraries of each institution. UCF materials are catalogued twice. The UCF Orlando campus library first catalogues materials for all UCF campuses, and then sends them to the regional campus library where they must be entered into the community college catalogue. UCF materials received at the joint-use library are then catalogued by a DBCC cataloguer. The double-cataloguing system results in delays in receiving items at the regional campus, and a wait to get items on the shelf once they are received in Daytona. However, after going through the protracted process, the volumes belonging to each institution are integrated on the shelves and students from either institution can check out any circulating books (Bozeman and Owens, 2007).

The management of the collection in a joint-use library is a complex undertaking. If two existing collections are to be merged, the amount of work this will require cannot be underestimated. In some joint-use libraries the partners maintain separate collections, often partly because the logistics of merging these proves too tricky to be overcome economically.

At Rockingham Regional Campus Community Library, before the tripartite agreement was formalised two library systems were used: one an automated Dynix system and the other a Browne manual system. This proved problematic, as each stakeholder group wanted to continue to use its own system. It was eventually decided it was in the best interests of all parties to use the Innopac library management system, which the university was already using, and now all three branches of the city of Rockingham are on the same system (Hamblin, 2007).

At the Metropolitan State University St Paul Campus in Minnesota, however, the university and public library sections have maintained different library management systems. This means that library users in one system also need to be registered in the other system, and users who wish to use both the university and the public library resources need two library cards. The same is true at the Alvin Sherman Library in Florida. In addition, here, as in several other joint-use public-academic libraries, both Library of Congress and Dewey classification systems are used, but MacDougall (2007) claims this is not a problem:

'the customer doesn't seem to care as long as they can find what they want'.

Even when both libraries operate the same library management system, merging catalogues is not a straightforward procedure. In Florida, both DBCC and UCF libraries use the ALEPH library management system, which is shared among all Florida community colleges through the College Center for Library Automation (CCLA). This allows any community college student to search the catalogues of all 28 community colleges in Florida. The state university libraries are also in the process of converting to the ALEPH system, and UCF has completed the conversion. However, there are no plans to link the community college and university systems. Community college students will not be able seamlessly to search the universities' catalogues, nor vice versa (Bozeman and Owens, 2007).

A further concern in the area of collection management in joint-use libraries is the disposal of stock. In a public library, stock is usually weeded from the collection when it ceases to be issued regularly or its appearance deteriorates so as to make it potentially off-putting to users. In an academic library, however, different criteria are adopted. Often the most sensible approach in a joint-use public-academic library is to have different weeding policies for the different areas of the collection.

Borrowing rights

Academic libraries usually operate a system of different borrowing rights for different types of user (e.g. undergraduates, postgraduates, staff). However, in a joint-use library there may need to be more distinctions between users with different needs. The number of items and loan periods usually vary for each category of user. Fines for overdue items can also be an area where practices differ. A school library may not charge for overdue items, for instance, while the public library service does. Practices need to be reconciled so as to be understandable for users.

Technology

In all types of library, the expansion of ICT resources means increasing pressure on space. This can be a particular problem in joint-use libraries if each partner requires its own network of PCs, perhaps for security reasons. The way in which ICT resources are used in joint-use libraries can differ significantly from use in a stand-alone library where there is greater homogeneity between the needs of users. In a joint-use university-public library, for instance, users will want access to PCs for e-mail and to find basic information, but there will also be significant numbers of users who will need access to a PC for much longer periods of time than the average public library user: a student typing up an assignment or a researcher carrying out a series of complex searches of a database, for instance. This means that there will need to be greater flexibility in terms of time periods and types of use than might be the case in a public library. At Metropolitan State University library, for example, community users are encouraged to work on two designated banks of computers, only using others if there is no conflict with student or faculty use (Barton et al., 2007).

Although in the vast majority of cases all resources in a joint-use library will be accessible to all users, there are exceptions, most notably some electronic resources which require licences. As the proportion of library collections which is provided in an electronic format continues to increase, it is likely that this will become even more problematic for joint-use libraries, unless new licensing models are developed.

Differences in the ethos of different library sectors can also be apparent in their respective attitudes towards the appropriate use of technology. While a library which is part of an educational institution may believe it is appropriate to prioritise use for educational purposes, a wider range of purposes may be legitimate in a public library.

Access

The question of whether it is acceptable to charge public library users for car-parking is an issue which has arisen in a number of joint-use libraries. At the Metropolitan State University in Minnesota, for instance, the library site was not large enough to provide adequate parking for the number of people anticipated to use the building. The university does operate a large pay-lot about half a city block away, but on-site parking is limited to 34 spaces – barely adequate for public library use most of the time. Initially, the university intended to install a pay system and charge patrons to park in the library parking lot. This was intended as a traffic management undertaking, not a revenue-enhancing venture. However, members of the city council and the local community objected to having to pay to park while visiting a public library, so this idea was scrapped in favour of using security staff already employed in the library to monitor the parking lot and issue tickets to anyone staying longer than an hour. While not perfect, this has proven to be a workable compromise (Barton et al., 2007).

At Rockingham Regional Campus Community Library in Western Australia, there were initially different arrangements for different types of users. University students paid for parking, TAFE students did not, and the city would never agree to charge for public parking. After years of energetic discussion the university decided to give free parking at Rockingham. However, even now there are still problems because the public parking is closer to the library than the student parking, and so students are still tempted to park there (Hamblin, 2007).

Conclusions

This chapter has explored how the basic functions of a library service operate in a joint-use environment. It is clear that there is no one answer and that compromise between the partners is essential. Operating a joint-use library is difficult, because it requires new ways of thinking and changes to traditional working practices. This can be worrying for staff, but attitudes within the library profession at all levels need to change in order to ensure the success of joint-use libraries. At present, too many library services are reluctant to relinquish control and librarians fear a loss of status. To overcome these fears, joint-use libraries need to be accepted as a credible form of library provision in their own right and, in particular, joint-use librarianship needs to be recognised and rewarded as a highly skilled career path which requires a complex range of skills.

Note

1. The Transfer of Undertakings (Protection of Employment) Regulations 1981 and 2006.

5

Joint-use libraries and partnerships

It is, of course, stating the obvious to say that partnerships are at the heart of any joint-use library. Without carefully managed, successful partnerships, the establishment and operation of an effective joint-use library are impossible. Differences, or a lack of understanding, between partners are probably the most common cause of 'failed' joint-use libraries.

In recent years there has been a strong emphasis on the importance of partnership working from governments and other policy-makers in various countries and library sectors. These include the UK Audit Commission (2002), the UK Museums, Archives and Libraries Council (2007), the UK Department for Education and Skills (2004a, 2004b), the UK Cabinet Office (2005), the Scottish Executive (2003a, 2004, 2007), Nova Scotia Economic Development (2006) and the Swedish government (IFLA, 1996), to name but a few. Although these policy documents rarely refer explicitly to libraries, they do indicate a strong interest generally in collaboration among policy-makers. These initiatives were discussed in greater detail in Chapter 2.

This chapter describes various types of potential partnerships, then moves on to discuss the advantages of partnership working, the obstacles to collaboration and success factors which have been established through previous research.

Building on firm foundations

A joint-use library is, of course, a major undertaking, and if it is the first project that the partner organisations have worked on together there will obviously be a lot of issues to be discussed and problems to overcome. In many cases, however, the decision to establish a joint-use library is the result of previous collaborations between the organisations involved, often stretching over a number of years. For example, prior to the establishment of the joint public-health library at Bolton Central Library, Bolton PCT and Bolton Libraries already collaborated very effectively with various initiatives such as distribution of health promotion leaflets through branch libraries, reciprocal membership schemes and the 'books on prescription' scheme.[1] The move to a joint library venue was seen as an opportunity to enhance such initiatives and expand areas for joint working (Hardman and Melmoth, 2007).

For many organisations which choose to establish a joint-use library, a general interest in partnership working is part of their ethos and way of working. For instance, Broward County Library developed a reputation for partnership working in the 1980s and 1990s, and had worked with over 500 community partners before the joint university-public Alvin Sherman Library was established (MacDougall, 2007).

Potential partners

There are a multitude of potential partnership options when creating a joint-use library. This reinforces the point that all joint-use libraries are unique, have their own individual aims and have to deal with very different issues. The most common forms of partnership involving libraries from different sectors were outlined in Chapter 1. However, there are also a number of other organisations which can be partners in joint-use library development. The permutations for possible partnerships are almost unlimited.

Community partners

Community groups are increasingly becoming involved in the running of public libraries. For example, in Buckinghamshire in the UK, when Iver and Richings Park libraries were closed in November 2006, Iver Community Libraries was formed with the aim of providing library services and other information resources in both Richings Park and Iver. Richings Park was opened in February 2007 and operates six days a week, 34 hours a week; it is staffed by volunteers and has a stock of over 2,000 books, including some reference, non-fiction and large print. The aim now is to incorporate a new community resource centre in a local shop in the vicinity of the old library. This shop is well used by older residents as a social centre. A room has been provided for the community resource centre in which the group hopes to include internet access as well as library facilities (Iver Community Libraries, 2007). Developments such as this have implications for joint-use libraries, a number of which already work closely with community groups.

Case study: Gipsyville, Hull, UK

In Hull the library service works with several community organisations, including Pickering and Newington Development Association (PANDA). The Gipsyville Library has been in existence since the 1950s, but in the 1990s government funding enabled the creation of a new multipurpose centre on the site, including health services, a jobshop, training rooms and meeting rooms as well as the library. The new centre, which opened in 1999, is managed by PANDA and the management board is composed of local residents and business people. The centre is staffed by PANDA employees.

In 2002 a review of library service points reported a low level of library usage at Gipsyville and the management board was concerned that the library would be closed. So in 2004 management of the library was transferred to PANDA to safeguard the resource for the community. The library is now managed through a service-level agreement which sets out the responsibilities of each partner for the operation of the service. The inclusion of local representatives on the library management board has enabled the community to have more involvement in service development, for example in stock forums and consultations on future developments.

The library budget for managing the service was transferred to PANDA to be managed by the centre manager. This funds additional staffing, utilities and general running costs. PANDA also provides financial input through obtaining external funding for service development. For example, between 2004 and 2006 PANDA secured funding to operate a jobshop from the library area.

Both the library service and PANDA are aware that achievements must be sustained to ensure that the library continues to improve. They are working together to secure funding to extend the building, improve the internal layout and create spacious zoned areas for activities and improved services to meet identified community needs. This includes a larger children's area, a performance space for cultural events, improved ICT facilities, a café and a community radio suite; the library service will be integrated with these other developments. The management board is encouraging more local people to participate on the board, to make it more representative of the local community. This will include a youth panel to represent the interests of local young people.

The partnership, management and staffing structure at Gipsyville have become a role model for other joint-use libraries in the city. Management of the partnership through the service-level agreement and management board gives the partners the flexibility to adapt services to meet changing community needs. The local community has an opportunity to be involved in service development and to take ownership of these developments, supporting the council's strategy for neighbourhood management of services. The increase in usage since the joint-use facility was created indicates that the library has a significant role to play in the future development of the community (Richmond, 2007).

Private sector partners

An increasing number of joint-use libraries are being conceived as public-private partnerships and funded by the Private Finance Initiative (PFI). In the UK, the PFI is now used to fund major new public building projects, including hospitals, schools, prisons and roads. The Conservatives first introduced the scheme in the early 1990s; under New Labour the PFI has become a major, and controversial, element of private sector involvement in Britain's public services.[2]

It is not just in the UK that publicly funded libraries are working with private companies to establish and run joint-use libraries. In China, Ke Ping (2001) reported that the East China Normal University Library worked with the Shanghai Dongfang Real Estate Company to build an advanced computer education centre which is open to the company for its technical needs while also being used as an electronic reading room for the entire campus.

Case study: Wootton Fields

Wootton Fields Library is England's first PFI joint-use library and is part of a complex of new community services which combine to make the Wooldale Centre for Learning. Mitie, a support service company which services, maintains, manages and improves buildings and infrastructure for a wide range of private and public sector customers, was brought in to manage the overall project and it subcontracted the establishment and management of the library to Tribal, a provider of consulting and professional support services.

Wootton, near Northampton, was rapidly outgrowing the existing public services in the area. There was an increase in demand for places at local schools, library access and other services for the community. In particular, new housing estates created a strong case for a new secondary school in the area. The result was the Wooldale Centre for Learning, which includes a new school for pupils aged between four and 18 years, a nursery and adult learning facilities.

Tribal supported Northampton library service with sourcing appropriate material, organising the layout of the library and preparing it ready for public use. In addition, the company recruited a team of library specialists to work on the Wootton Fields site and within the Northamptonshire libraries network. This ongoing management will continue for 25 years (Beveridge, 2007).

Sure Start

Sure Start has been involved in a number of joint-use libraries in the UK. It is a government programme which aims to achieve better outcomes for children, parents and communities by:

- increasing the availability of childcare for all children;
- improving health and emotional development for young children;
- supporting parents as parents and in their aspirations towards employment.[3]

Sure Start children's centres are places where children under five years old and their families can receive integrated services and information, and access help from multidisciplinary teams of professionals. One of the services offered is information and advice to parents and carers on a range of subjects, including local childcare, looking after babies and young children, local early-years provision (childcare and early learning) and education services for three- and four-year-olds.

Case study: Sunshine Library, Wakefield

The Sunshine Library in Wakefield is the first purpose-built early-years library in the UK, and provides a focus for early language development and book enjoyment among families living in the deprived community of Sure Start Wakefield West. Its development came about through the shared vision of Wakefield Library Services, St George's Community Project and Sure Start, and the enthusiasm of the early-years librarian.

The library is open every day, supported by a member of staff and trained volunteers. There is a strong emphasis on outreach activity to encourage parents who have not been inside a library before. The Sunshine Library runs 'Busy Babies' and 'Messy Monkeys', which are short courses run by the Workers' Educational Association (WEA) offering parents and very young children craft activities, storytelling sessions and help in choosing books to borrow. 'Cyber Tots' are individual sessions run with young children to help them access CD-ROMs or use word-processing packages.

The library is housed next door to St George's Under Twos Nursery, which provides opportunities for shared activities and, for the nursery, access to book loans to support special themes. The library offers a 'tea and tissues' session first thing in the morning to provide a listening ear for parents who are getting used to leaving their children for the very first time, and to encourage them to see the library as a resource they can access. Upstairs is an adult training centre.

Parents were involved in the design of the nursery from the very beginning, in the appointment of staff, the library theme (the farmyard), designing the Bookstart[4] Plus bags and even the choice of name. At a strategic level, libraries have a high profile within Wakefield Council, which has enabled long-term support for their work. The strong partnership has led to confidence in obtaining long-term mainstream funding for the Sunshine Library and its work (National Literacy Trust, 2007).

Council services

The concept of 'one-stop shops' or customer service centres has grown in popularity in recent years as a means by which local councils provide residents with a range of services – typically housing advice, bill payments, bus-pass and parking-permit applications, environmental services, trading standards and councillors' surgeries as well as access via telephone or a kiosk to other council services. In many authorities, libraries have partnered with other council services in one-stop shops.

Case study: Blackburn Connected

In January 2007 West Lothian Council launched its first integrated library and customer service centre, called Blackburn Connected. This employs generic staff delivering all services from one location and acting as a first point of contact for a range of services. The project was initiated in response to a number of pressures on council facilities in the Blackburn area. Customer traffic had been falling in the customer service centre (CSC); at the same time, book issues were also decreasing and the library was in need of refurbishment. Partnership between the two service areas has resulted in a new integrated service, which delivers:

- extended-hours access to all council services at first point of contact;
- a purpose-built facility designed around local need;
- access to housing services staff;
- surgeries with local elected members;
- appointment system with Benefits Agency staff;
- access to revenue services via 'tele talk', a video link to a revenue officer who provides information and help with enquiries about housing benefit, council tax benefit, council tax and rent;
- a credit union accommodated within the building;
- increased free access to PCs for adult learning, an internet café and study areas;
- improved links with schools for formal class visits;

- trained staff to assist customers in their use of online functions e.g. booking service, payments;

- tailored programme of visits for local special-needs school students;

- adult reading groups;

- organised activities for teenagers aiming to reduce disorder in the community caused by young people.

The partnership model has proved successful and is now being considered for the delivery of mobile services to take council services to some of the harder-to-reach communities, with the potential of working in partnership with other services including the Benefits Bus, debt and welfare support and links to health through the health improvement team (Brough, 2007).

Tourist information

Tourist information centres (TICs) provide information to the public and local businesses about tourist attractions, events, accommodation, transport and other facilities in the region and nationwide. It is not uncommon for TICs to be housed in the same building as the library, or indeed to be integrated into a public library. An example is Bolton tourist information centre, which has been based at the Central Library since 2005. This is described in Chapter 1.

Primary Care Trusts

The UK's Department of Health is working towards a 'patient-led NHS' (Department of Health, 2005), which means there is a need for the general public to make informed choices about their health and lifestyle.

Increasingly, the public are also being asked for their opinions and ideas on how NHS services should function. To fulfil these needs there is a requirement on PCTs to provide up-to-date, relevant, easily accessible health information for communities.

Case study: Bolton Public Library and Bolton PCT Learning and Resource Library

In January 2007 Bolton PCT Learning and Resource Library moved to new premises within Bolton Central Library. This new joint-use development, which took approximately two years to plan and implement, is now seen as an example of good practice in how local services can work proactively and jointly to provide quality customer-focused services. Following the success of the joint-use library, planned initiatives for the future include:

- healthy lifestyle sessions, e.g. health trainers will use the library as a venue to offer healthy lifestyle interventions to encourage members of the public to improve their health and well-being;
- health campaigns – possible flu clinics, mental health awareness and cancer-screening events;
- using the mobile library as a venue for health trainers to deliver their healthy lifestyle sessions within the wider community, especially around the disadvantaged areas in the borough (Hardman and Melmoth, 2007).

Youth and children's services

A number of youth and children's services have worked with public libraries to provide joint-use facilities targeted towards children and young people.

Case study: Tonge children's centre

Funding for the expansion of children's centres has enabled Bolton Libraries to work in partnership with Children's Services to meet the literacy and language development needs of parents and children aged under five. The latest children's centre in Bolton opened in May 2006, and includes a small library facility with picture books and adult non-fiction to support classes for parents being run in the centre. Sure Start monies also funded a one-year post to promote and develop the library; when the funding expired in March 2007, information assistants within the centre took on responsibility for the day-to-day running of the library. The facility has proved popular with parents and has helped the library service to target hard-to-reach groups.

Case study: The Moss Side Powerhouse Library, Manchester

The Moss Side Powerhouse is a centre for nine- to 25-year-olds: it has a youth library where young people can use computers, get help with their homework at the homework zone, borrow books and CDs, read magazines or relax with their friends. The Powerhouse also has youth clubs, a Connexions[5] advice centre and a sports hall and recording studio. There are events and activities ranging from sports to music and recording projects, arts and crafts and trips out during the holidays.

Adult learning

For many years adult learning providers have used public library facilities to deliver courses and support students. However, in some joint-use libraries this arrangement has become more formalised. This issue is discussed in more depth in Chapter 7.

Charities

Charities which provide information services are another possible joint-use partner for libraries.

For example, the Age Concern Library in Leicester, UK, is a unique partnership between the local authority library service and the charity Age Concern. It caters specifically for the over-55s in its stock, services and facilities, while still being part of a public library network (Leicester City Council, undated). The CAB service, which helps people resolve their legal, money and other problems by providing free information and advice, is another charity which might be co-located with a library. In early 2007, for example, Sunbury CAB in Surrey moved from a day centre to Sunbury library. This was felt to be the best option for the library service because use had been declining significantly in recent years and this move is considered a positive way of increasing footfall and prominence in the locality (Spelthorne Borough Council, 2006).

As stated in Chapter 1, this book focuses on partnerships between libraries and other information providers. However, it is worth remembering that, in the provision of joint-use facilities, libraries often form partnerships with a variety of other bodies, including cultural organisations (e.g. theatres), leisure providers (e.g. leisure centre, swimming pool) and caterers (e.g. onsite café).

Collaboration between public and education libraries

The above examples illustrate the sheer range of possibilities for partnerships in a joint-use library. However, it still remains the case that the majority of joint-use libraries involve a public library and one or more educational institutions. It is therefore worth reflecting on a piece of research carried out in 2002 which investigated collaboration between libraries and education (McNicol et al., 2002). This considered a variety of types of collaborative arrangements, including resource sharing, access arrangements, joint ICT, cooperative staff training and joint promotion. The report found a number of potential advantages of collaborative ventures for public and academic libraries, and also for learners, including being a way to reach new learners, more flexible course delivery options, shared catalogues, joint funding opportunities, raising the profile of both organisations, sharing of skills and expertise and an opportunity to exchange ideas and solve problems. However, there were also difficulties to be overcome, namely staff attitudes, lack of time, lack of commitment, incompatibility of systems, different aims and objectives and different working practices. In general, cross-sectoral and cross-domain links were felt to be difficult to establish and maintain because of poor communication and a lack of understanding of each other's aims and way of working. The key factors identified for a successful collaboration were good planning, management and evaluation, commitment, communication and high-level support.

Many of these advantages, difficulties and success factors are identical to those found in the literature on joint-use libraries. The main opportunities, obstacles and success factors in relation to partnership working in joint-use libraries are discussed in the remainder of this chapter.

Opportunities

Partnership working in joint-use libraries offers some distinct advantages over single-sector stand-alone libraries, including reduced costs, increased usage, longer opening hours, better use of specialist skills, access to alternative funding streams and new insights.

Reduced costs

Of course, one potential opportunity offered by joint-use library partnership is cost saving. This might be achieved through shared building costs and overheads, cheaper access to specialist services or more efficient use of resources. One example is the Blackburn Connected project in West Lothian, where relocating the library released land with a potential value of £250,000. The money from the sale of this land was used to fund the refurbishment of the new facility. In addition, the project involved the relocation of a post office, which resulted in a cash saving. In total, it was calculated that the relocation of the library saved £150,000 in maintenance costs (Brough, 2007). However, when carrying out these types of calculations, it needs to be remembered that partnership working brings its own costs – for instance, time commitment and more complex communication structures.

Increased library usage

Libraries from all sectors are concerned about declining usage in the face of competition from other information sources, changes in lifestyles and similar developments. The potential to increase library usage is often cited as a possible benefit of a joint-use library partnership. It can be a way for each partner to attract new users. If they are co-located with other services, joint-use libraries can be an effective way for public libraries to reach traditionally 'hard-to-reach' groups. Similarly, a joint academic-public library can help a college or university to recruit students who might normally be deterred from attending a formal education institution, thus helping to widen participation. This issue is discussed in greater detail in Chapter 7.

The evidence from many joint-use libraries would seem to suggest that they do, indeed, lead to greater usage. At The Bridge in Glasgow, since merging with John Wheatley College the public library has climbed the league table from 24th in terms of issues to being consistently in the top five and often second only to Glasgow's Hillhead library (which is situated in arguably the best-educated constituency in Britain). In the first six months of operation, compared to the previous college and public library totals:

- the service issued 26 per cent more items;

- adult non-fiction issues rose by 57 per cent, and this rise was consistently higher than the previous college library issues (on average approximately 200 per cent), demonstrating a higher usage of the service by college students than previously;

- teenage items which had been in decline in the original public service, with issues down approximately 50 per cent compared to the equivalent month the year before, increased substantially after the service change, up by approximately 50 per cent for each month;

- adult fiction issues decreased for the first few months but then recovered as older users adjusted to the new environment;

- the number of PC taster sessions used as a lead-in to the college's flexible learning sessions increased by 21 per cent;

- junior fiction (91 per cent) and non-fiction (30 per cent) issues both substantially increased over the previous period;

- while PC usage was not recorded for the previous college service, for an increase of five PCs there has been an increase of 146 per cent in PC usage compared to the previous public service (Kearney, 2007).

Likewise, at Gipsyville in Hull the number of active borrowers as a percentage of the ward population increased from 8.3 per cent in March 2004 to 10.5 per cent in March 2007. In comparison, the city average remained static throughout the same period (Richmond, 2007).

However, loan statistics are not always a good indicator for joint-use libraries. For example, members of the public may be the heaviest borrowers, but academic users are likely to require more staff time in dealing with reference enquiries. It is therefore important that, when attempting to measure usage of a joint-use library, a range of measures are collected to give a truer picture of the impact of a joint-use facility on library use.

Longer opening hours

For many joint-use libraries, the provision of longer opening hours is seen as one of the main benefits for the local community. This can happen in many different types of library. For example, a joint-use library in a remote rural area can offer extended hours compared to a part-time branch library or mobile service; a joint school-public library means that students have access to the library throughout the school year, not just during term-time; and a joint academic-public library is likely to be open for longer in the evenings than most equivalent stand-alone public libraries, possibly 24 hours a day. However, although extended opening hours are usually an advantage of joint-use provision, in some school-public libraries opening hours for the public can be curtailed at times when the school has exclusive use of the library.

Making the best use of specialist skills

As well as being efficient in terms of the use of resources, joint-use libraries provide a means of making the best use of specialist skills among the staff from all the partners. This might mean, for example, that librarians from an academic library provide information skills training for members of the public, while reader development staff from the public library run reading groups to encourage students to read more widely. This sharing of skills also applies to other partner organisations. So, for instance, early-years or youth workers can offer services to engage these groups in the library. As well as directly providing services for users, specialist staff can offer training and advice to colleagues to help improve the way in which all library staff support particular user needs.

Access to new funding streams

Partnerships are also a way to access new funding streams which would not normally be open to a particular type of library. For example, a UK public library may benefit from extended schools[6] funding through partnering with a school or Learning and Skills Council[7] funding via a partnership with a college.

Fresh ideas and insights

This potential benefit of joint-use libraries is often overlooked, but it should not be forgotten that working in partnership offers tremendous opportunities to discuss issues in order to gain new insights and benefit from fresh ideas and approaches. The problems of bringing together organisations with different ways of working are well rehearsed in the literature. However, the fact that partners have differing outlooks, experiences and professional backgrounds can be a distinct advantage when seeking novel solutions to problems and looking for ways to improve services.

Obstacles

There are, of course, often obstacles to partnership working which can prove tricky to overcome.

Staff attitudes

A lack of understanding, or commitment, from staff can be one of the greatest barriers to effective joint-use libraries, and one of the hardest to overcome. The difficulties of convincing staff who have spent their entire careers in a single library sector of the benefits of partnership working were described in Chapter 4. And some library staff may be even more reluctant to engage with those from other professional backgrounds.

Lack of commitment

It is sometimes the case that one partner is more committed to the concept of a joint-use library than another. Unequal levels of commitment can be problematic and can cause difficulties at all levels, from senior managers to front-line staff. The concept of a joint-use library has to be embraced by all partner organisations and not just seen as a stop-gap solution, or even a last resort, when faced with a problem such as severe budget reductions.

Different aims and objectives

Of course, the partners involved will each have their own aims and objectives, and these will differ. However, it is imperative that they also have shared core aims which can act as a focus for the joint-use library. Above all, they should share a commitment to partnership working. Essentially, the partners in a joint-use library should concentrate on those areas where they share mutual interest, rather than highlighting differences. Two of these are suggested in the following chapters: lifelong learning and inclusion are aims which can be shared by most public sector and voluntary bodies. So, for instance, while university libraries may be more concerned with formal educational opportunities and public libraries see their role as providing informal learning, they can complement each other and offer a range of options which meet the needs of different users in a joint-use library.

Incompatibility of systems

At a practical level, joint-use libraries often experience difficulties when trying to bring together two or more different systems, which in many instances have been established for a number of years. This is especially problematic when trying to bring together two library management systems. Indeed, a number of joint-use libraries find they are unable to achieve a single catalogue and have to maintain separate systems. There are numerous other examples: bringing together two or more financial systems, practices for ordering and processing stock and methods of arranging materials are just a few examples. These are not insurmountable, although compromises will need to be made. Often, rather than one partner adapting to the systems used by another, a new solution, and one which works best for a joint-use library rather than either of the individual partners, needs to be found.

Different working practices

The same applies to different working practices. Adapting to new ways of working can be unsettling, but ultimately examining existing practices can lead to a better solution which benefits both staff and users. Observing how other professions and organisations work and reflecting on existing practice have obvious benefits. A common problem when working with partners from different professional backgrounds is that there are differences in language and terms used which can lead to misunderstanding. All sides need to make efforts to appreciate the working methods and expertise of other partners and take the best elements from each to create a new way of working.

Success factors

The key success factors for partnership working, both in joint-use libraries and more widely, are a shared vision; an equivalent or better level of service; senior-level support; commitment throughout the organisation; good planning, management and evaluation; and effective communication.

A shared vision

The partners need to agree on a shared vision for the joint-use facility. This should inspire and motivate partners, and it needs to be strong enough to overcome traditions, competition and fears about loss of identity.

The ability to provide a level of service equal to, or better than, that provided in separate facilities

There must be real benefits for all parties in a joint-use library partnership; this includes not only all the organisations involved, but also their users. The purpose of a partnership arrangement is to improve the way in which services are provided for users and the ways in which organisations operate. So if the service provided by any partner is compromised then the partnership ceases to be of value. At the start of the partnership, all parties need to identify how they will benefit from the arrangement and this needs to be set out in a formal document and constantly monitored.

High-level support

Any partnership agreement, and especially a major undertaking such as a joint-use library, requires high-level support from senior managers and leaders in each of the organisations involved. The partnership needs to correspond with the missions and strategies of the organisations and the interests of those in influential positions. The significance of individual personalities involved in the development of a joint-use library was discussed in Chapter 2, and the importance of securing genuine commitment at the highest levels should not be underestimated.

Commitment at all levels

Support for the concept of a joint-use library partnership at a high level in the organisations involved is not sufficient in itself; this support needs to permeate the whole service. All staff have to be committed to the idea of a joint-use facility and enthusiastic about the potential benefits in order for the partnership to succeed. Most importantly, there needs to be a commitment to cultural change to support the adjustments which will be necessary for all involved. Furthermore, staff at all levels in the partner organisations need to have a commitment to ongoing learning and development and be open to new ideas.

Good planning, management and evaluation

Good planning, management and evaluation are naturally essential for any successful partnership. These points are supported throughout the literature on joint-use libraries. In particular, the importance of the agreement which sets out how the partnership will operate, and if necessary be dissolved, is seen as key. The agreement should include plans for space, staffing, information technology, the governing body and evaluation.

Communication

Finally, effective communication is required. This includes communication between senior decision-makers and staff; between the organisations and their users; and between the staff in each organisation to allow the sharing of knowledge and expertise. In each case, communication needs to be a two-way process, not just an information-giving exercise.

However, it needs to be recognised that developing and maintaining effective communication and understanding between professionals from different library services and beyond require time and patience.

Conclusions

Partnerships are at the heart of any joint-use library. If the partnership fails, then the library will fail. However, it is in this area that joint-use libraries, perhaps, have the greatest potential to lead the way for other types of library. Many joint-use libraries are exploring innovative models of working and new forms of collaboration; the lessons learnt through this activity will have relevance well beyond joint-use libraries. Indeed, many joint-use libraries are looked to as models of partnership working within their wider organisations or local area. However, the time and effort required to maintain partnerships cannot be underestimated. Inevitably there will be disagreements, but what is crucial is that these are confronted, not ignored. The constant monitoring and evaluation of the joint-use partnership are one of the most important aspects of joint-use library evaluation, as discussed in Chapter 8. From research into joint-use libraries and other areas, much is known about the potential problems and the factors which make for a successful partnership. Putting this knowledge into practice in the real world, however, is often far from easy.

Notes

1. See www.bolton.nhs.uk/services/socialprescribing/projects/Books. pdf.

2. For more details see www.hm-treasury.gov.uk/documents/public_ private_partnerships/ppp_index.cfm.

3. See www.surestart.gov.uk/.

4. See www.bookstart.co.uk/.

5. Connexions provides information and advice about careers, health, legal issues, relationships, finance etc. for 13–19-year-olds.

6. As a key way of delivering *Every Child Matters* outcomes, an extended school works with the local authority, local providers and other schools to provide access to a core offer of integrated services: a varied range of activities including study support, sport and music clubs, combined with childcare in primary schools, parenting and family support, swift and easy access to targeted and specialist services, community access to facilities including adult and family learning, ICT and sports grounds. These will often be provided beyond the school day, but not necessarily by teachers or on the school site.

7. The LSC is responsible for planning and funding high-quality education and training for everyone in England other than those in universities.

6

Joint-use libraries and communities

Joint-use libraries can be seen as naturally inclusive organisations; they open up facilities to a wider audience and make services and resources available to groups who would normally be denied access. For instance, a joint-use university-public library makes a wide range of specialist resources, which would not normally be provided in a public library, available to any member of the public. This ethos is one that fits well with contemporary concerns for social justice throughout the world, and the work being done in this area within the joint-use library sector may provide models for other libraries, information services and similar organisations.

The idea of social inclusion is particularly important to public libraries. It has been central to their mission for more than a decade, and even prior to this many public libraries made efforts to provide services for disadvantaged groups and reach out to local communities, although they may not have used the term 'social inclusion'. Over time, initiatives have become more sophisticated and targeted as libraries have devised new ways of working with and providing services for groups such as children in the care of local authorities, lesbians, gay men, bisexuals and transgendered people (LGBT), ethnic minority populations and, most recently, refugees, asylum-seekers and guest workers.[1] This often involves libraries working with partner organisations which have a more detailed knowledge of the needs of such groups.

As Buiskool et al. (2005: 193) commented: 'Public libraries are seen as accessible places... accessible to broad groups of the population, including those who might otherwise be excluded.'

The research work on UK libraries, published as *Open to All?* (Resource, 2000), showed that in 1998–1999 most public libraries were using social inclusion policies developed within their local authorities, often based on anti-poverty or equality work. However, three years later *Framework for the Future* challenged libraries to 're-double their efforts to reach non-users'. It confirmed that: 'Libraries are public anchors for neighbourhoods and communities. For the majority of the population, libraries are acknowledged as safe, welcoming, neutral spaces open to all in the community' (Department for Culture, Media and Sport, 2003: 38). But, significantly for joint-use libraries, the document pointed out that one route to non-users is through collaboration with other public services, for example by co-locating public libraries with services such as education, social services, health or leisure services.

Some definitions

The term 'social exclusion' was first used in France in 1974, and during the following 30 years it spread through EU policy and research channels. The European Social Fund's definition of social inclusion is: 'The development of capacity and opportunity to play a full role, not only in economic terms, but also in social, psychological and political terms' (cited in Centre for Economic & Social Inclusion, undated).

Explaining social inclusion in more practical terms, the UK government defines it as follows:

> Social inclusion is achieved when individuals or areas do not suffer from the negative effects of unemployment, poor skills, low income, poor housing, crime, bad health, family problems, limited access to services and rurality, e.g. remoteness, sparsity, isolation and high costs. (Cited in Centre for Economic & Social Inclusion, undated)

In the twenty-first century the idea of community cohesion has become increasingly important. The definition of community cohesion (drawn from the Cantle Report[2]) currently used by the government and other agencies gives a strong sense that cohesion is wider and deeper than other similar initiatives (such as tackling social exclusion, diversity, equality work). It has been stated that 'Community cohesion incorporates and goes beyond the concept of race equality and social inclusion' (Office of the Deputy Prime Minister, 2003).

The broad working definition is that a cohesive community is one where:

- there is a common vision and a sense of belonging for all communities;
- the diversity of people's different backgrounds and circumstances is appreciated and positively valued;
- those from different backgrounds have similar life opportunities;
- strong and positive relationships are being developed between people from different backgrounds in the workplace, in schools and within neighbourhoods (The Network, 2006).

The 'Making a difference' report, which set out to identify ways to tackle poverty, pointed out: 'Community cohesion depends on there being "neutral" public places to which people can go' (Department for Work and Pensions, 2006). The notion of libraries as 'third places' is clearly important when considering their role in community cohesion. In 1989 Ray Oldenburg published a study of 'hangouts at the heart of the community' – local places 'that help to get you through the day'. He uses the term 'third places', distinguishing these from the home and the workplace, and he stresses their neutrality: the fact that visitors are not encumbered by the role of either host or guest. He notes also that those who enter third places enter a genuinely casual environment.

Joint-use libraries and social inclusion

How can joint-use libraries make a contribution to combating social exclusion? As mentioned above, implementing social inclusion policies usually involves libraries working in partnership, something which is central to a joint-use library. A common criticism of many social inclusion initiatives is that they are project-based, and therefore of finite length, rather than mainstreamed, sustainable services. In contrast to such an approach, the standard services provided as a matter of course in a joint-use library exemplify the principles of social inclusion on an ongoing basis. In essence, they 'open up' libraries and information services such as university, school and health libraries which normally restrict access to a defined user group. In addition, many joint-use libraries involve a partner from outside the library sector, such as a children's information service, CAB or community information service. A joint-use library therefore provides an opportunity for the approaches to social inclusion from different sectors to be combined and further developed.

In addition to their general role in improving access to information and library services, many joint-use libraries target services at particular groups which can be seen as excluded. The following are two examples of such targeted services.

Serving rural populations

Traditionally, joint-use libraries have been predominantly sited in rural areas. They provide access to books, ICT resources and other library services for people who would not otherwise have easy access to such facilities because of distance and poor transport links. They can thus help to ensure equality of opportunity between urban and rural communities. Often the alternative to a joint-use school-public library is a mobile service which visits infrequently, or even no public library at all within the community. This, of course, causes most difficulty for those who are experiencing other problems, such as low income or illness, which make them unable to travel to the nearest large centre of population. A joint-use library can help to sustain rural communities, providing library, information, education and allied services which can help to ensure local people remain in the community. A good example of this is the UHI Millennium Institute in Scotland, which has learning centres in many libraries in the Highlands and Islands offering access to university education to inhabitants of highly isolated communities.

Another example can be found in the Northwestern Territories of Canada, where a community libraries project is providing a library service for communities without libraries in an area where literacy levels are low, there is no access to bookstores and many residents cannot afford to buy books. The communities selected for inclusion in this project have a high level of community involvement and an interest in literacy programmes. Library staff are provided with training in community literacy, which includes storytelling, developing activities around a story and rhymes with a northern theme (Hopkins and Turner, 2006).

Case study: Ardnamurchan Library

The Ardnamurchan and Morvern ward in the Scottish Highlands has a total population of just over 2,000, 12.9 per cent of whom are aged between five and 14. However, there are relatively few young adults: approximately half the population is aged 44 or over, 10 per cent higher than the average for Scotland. Eighteen per cent of the population can speak, read or write Gaelic; significantly higher than the average for Scotland as a whole.

Ardnamurchan High School is a new school which was opened in September 2002. It was intended to be 'a nucleus for the whole community, offering educational, sporting, leisure and cultural opportunities for all ages, allowing young people to stay in their community' (Scottish Executive, 2003b).

Previously, pupils had faced daily journeys of up to three hours to travel to school and many had boarded. Local people had been campaigning for a school for more than a decade. In 2002–2003 there were 48 pupils, mainly S1 and S2 (12–14-year-olds), although there are also a few older pupils. In 2003–2004 the number rose to approximately 70, and it is hoped that eventually the roll will build up to around 150 pupils. There are still a small number of pupils who have to travel considerable distances to reach the school, and these board in the school's residence.

Ardnamurchan Library opened in November 2002, a few months after the school. Facilities available to both pupils and public users include a reference section, study area, resource collection, local collection, careers library, fiction and non-fiction, audio books, large-print books, DVDs/videos, newspapers, magazines and requests for Highland Council stock and titles obtained through inter-library loan. There are also photocopying facilities, two People's Network[3] computers and a coffee bar in the community area adjacent to the library. The library is open a total of 41 hours a week, considerably longer than many comparable community libraries. A quote from one public library user at Ardnamurchan illustrates its potential to support this rural community: 'the set up is brilliant... it shows the way ahead for the future... it's superb, what libraries ought to be, a real community centre' (McNicol, 2003).

Services for disabled users

Working in partnership and creating an accessible environment are two of the most important characteristics of joint-use libraries, and these are also crucial aspects of serving disabled users in any type of library (Council for Museums, Libraries and Archives, 2004). For instance, a welcoming entrance area, effective signage and easy external approach to the library are particularly important for disabled users. Beyond these general principles, there are a few examples of joint-use libraries which have created services specifically aimed at users with disabilities.

Case study: Papworth Everard Library

Papworth Everard Library has been built to serve the Cambridgeshire village community of Papworth and clients of the Papworth Trust, a registered charity that helps disabled people to be more independent. Before this library was built, the local community was served by a mobile unit. In fact, the library can be seen as the first real community building within the village. The objective was to offer library service provision to the entire community, as well as acting as a teaching library for disabled people to give them an opportunity to gain experience and qualifications in library work. Disabled people on the Papworth Progression Programme work alongside staff from the library service. The library has a range of specialist equipment, including screen readers, Braille software and magnifiers. There is a training library, primarily run by disabled people, which serves both disabled people and the wider community. The site shares space with the Disabled Living Centre, the Disability Information Service and several commercial organisations that deal with disabilities. Because the potential to be seen solely as a disability service within the community might be a barrier to able-bodied users, coffee mornings and open days are held to bring both elements of the community together (Cambridgeshire Libraries & Information Service, 2005).

Joint-use libraries and community cohesion

In addition to helping to combat social exclusion, joint-use libraries present an opportunity to make a substantial contribution to community cohesion, providing they develop a common vision and a sense of belonging for all members, and appreciate and positively value the diversity of people's backgrounds and circumstances. They certainly help to ensure similar life opportunities for those from different backgrounds by providing equality of access to information, reading and educational materials to those who would otherwise find it difficult to access such resources. This happens in a variety of ways: for example access for the public to specialist academic resources in a joint university-public library, or access for students in isolated areas to a wider range of reading materials through the public library's inter-library loan service. Informally, many joint-use library staff report strong and positive relationships being developed between people from different backgrounds.

This can be evident even in the smallest joint-use school-public library, where members of the community, especially older inhabitants, and students develop a better understanding of each other's viewpoints and needs through coming together in the shared environment of the library. Interestingly, according to Ruth Kifer (2007), one of the motivations behind the Dr Martin Luther King Jr joint-use library in San José was to improve the poor relationship that had existed between the university and the city. One way in which joint-use libraries regularly support cohesion is through involvement in shared community activities and events. To give just a one example, in 2007 the Alvin Sherman Library in Florida held an exhibition entitled 'The Jews of Czestochowa', featuring the Polish town of the Black Madonna. After an opening reception for over 200 community members of Jewish and Polish descent, members of the senior population brought their families to view this exhibition (MacDougall, 2007).

Case study: Charles Darwin University, Alice Springs Campus

The Alice Springs Campus of Charles Darwin University in the Northern Territory of Australia provides a joint-use library service for three educational sectors: higher education (HE), vocational education and training (VET) and secondary schools. There has always been difficulty with encouraging indigenous students to progress from Year 10, the last year of compulsory schooling in Australia, to HE. In the past, leaving town to do further study meant young people had to leave their family, their support system and their country – the land with which they identify. Feeling comfortable on campus may encourage seamless progression of Year 10s to HE. There is therefore a continual need to improve services to indigenous students in the library.

The collection has a strong indigenous slant, covering central Australian Aboriginal art, bush tucker, languages, history and culture. The library purchases everything written by local authors and/or published in Alice Springs. There is also a good collection of local and national magazines and newspapers. Material relating to Australian indigenous people is identified by a sticker of the Aboriginal flag attached to the spine. To make the environment more supportive for indigenous students and encourage them to make better use of it, ten Aboriginal artworks have been acquired and placed around the library. Many of the artists are based in Alice Springs, making it even more relevant to the students. There is also an ongoing display of Aboriginal books in the foyer of the library.

In addition, the library is building a collection of ESL (English as a second language) material as well as graphic novels to try to address literacy issues. The majority of indigenous students speak English as a second language at best, as each cultural group has its own language and will often speak other Australian indigenous languages as well.

It is recognised that recruiting Aboriginal staff will help to serve the needs of Aboriginal students better and make the library a more comfortable place for them to be. Indigenous staff are hard to find and keep, mainly because the family and cultural demands made on them conflict with the demands of the workplace. However, at present there are two casual staff in the library who identify as being Aboriginal (Sumner and Mamtora, 2007).

Case study: Dr Martin Luther King Library, San José

Ruth Kifer (2007) states that, according to a recent Pew research report, Hispanics with lower levels of education and English proficiency remain largely disconnected from the internet. Although internet usage is consistently low for all people with lower levels of education regardless of race, a much larger percentage of Hispanic adults have not finished high school than is the case for the population as a whole. Although Latino students make up 33 per cent of California's public high school graduates, only 16 per cent of Latino students are eligible for the University of California and only 7 per cent are eligible for the California State University system. The challenge for San José is to provide access to higher education for the growing and diverse population.

One of the 'learning pathway' portals offered by the King Library website is a multicultural gateway. This has information about language collections, events, special collections and links to 'websites for our diverse community', including local ESL classes, ethnic groups and cultures, immigration, disabilities, and gay, lesbian, bisexual and transgendered persons. Information is provided in Spanish, Chinese and Vietnamese as well as English. There are approximately 58,000 books in 58 languages in the collection, and over 40 languages are represented in the collection of entertainment and educational videos. The library also frequently holds multicultural events such as readings by authors, craft activities, music and storytelling.

Case study: North Regional/BCC Library

North Regional/BCC Library is both a Broward County library and a campus library for Broward Community College North Campus. It offers cultural programmes such as the Ruth E. Cohan Jewish Book Review series. There are also language support programmes: 'Kids Learn Spanish' introduces children to learning a second language; 'The English Café' is an informal conversational practice ground for adults who wish to improve their English-speaking skills; and 'El Club de Conversación en Español' invites adult English speakers to enhance their ability to speak and understand Spanish. Special programmes of interest to the deaf community have included an American Sign Language Literacy Festival and a visit by Miss Deaf America. Another planned initiative is 'Brazil ao Vivo', which will welcome children of Brazilian heritage and introduce their families to the library's services. Community members may increase their computer skills through hands-on classes in English, Spanish, Portuguese and Haitian Creole (Broward County Board of County Commissioners, undated:b).

Case study: African-American collections and services at the African-American Research Library and Cultural Center in Florida

The African-American Research Library and Cultural Center is a general-service library, as well as a research facility and cultural centre containing more than 75,000 books and related materials that focus on the experiences of people of African descent. There are literary collections of African-American authors; books and artefacts from

Africa, the Caribbean and North and South America; a small business resource centre; a career information resource area; exhibits, seminars and special events, including the Pan African Bookfest, Jazzteenth and Kwanzaa; and information on local history and a museum (Broward County Board of County Commissioners, undated:a).

Community engagement

Perhaps more than any other type of library, joint-use libraries need to engage with their user communities, and potential user communities, to ensure that they meet the needs of all groups. In the UK, improving the level of involvement of local people in public services is a major part of the government's modernisation agenda.

The three main forms of engagement are listed below.

- *Information gathering*: the collection of information about public attitudes and requirements through surveys, etc. There is no ongoing dialogue between the public and the organisation seeking the information. The public usually participate in this as individuals.

- *Consultation*: members of the public and the organisation work together for a defined period to discuss a particular policy or service issue. The methods used can range from focus groups to citizens' juries. People are brought together as representatives of the demographic profile of a particular community.

- *Participation*: members of the public and the organisation work together on an ongoing basis on a range of policy or service issues. These tend to focus on the community rather than on individuals. Community forums are an example.

Participation can be further divided into:

- *deciding together*: views are shared, options are generated jointly and a course of action is decided upon;

- *acting together*: working with others to make decisions and carry through the action agreed;

- *supporting local initiatives*: supporting independent groups to develop and implement their own solutions (London Councils, 2006).

However, community engagement can be a challenge. The following examples illustrate some ways in which joint-use libraries have engaged in all three forms of community engagement.

Case study: information gathering in West Lothian

The Blackburn Connected project in West Lothian undertook extensive community profiling work to identify over 30 community groups, local businesses and public sector partners. A detailed community engagement programme was agreed and implemented by the project team. The team were always clear that, rather than consultation, this was in fact extensive community information gathering and engagement. It was critical to win over the community by demonstrating the value of the joint-use facility, and the information-gathering activities helped the council to describe how it would operate to the benefit of the local community – such as by giving extended access to all council services under one roof and providing a new fit-for-purpose library resource handling everything from borrowing books and DVDs to bus-pass and transport enquiries, housing and revenue services. In addition, the protection of business for the local post office by transferring cash collections was found to be a major selling point (Brough, 2007).

Case study: consultation in Bolton

In 2005 Bolton Libraries undertook an externally funded arts-led research project to consult with the local community about a proposal to demolish an existing library and replace it with a new building. The library in question was in a disadvantaged area of Bolton with a large Asian population. Bolton Libraries was aware that the community might be alienated by traditional consultation methods such as questionnaires and focus groups. As an alternative, it tested new and innovative ways of consulting with culturally diverse communities.

Following a period of planning, training and induction five local artists, all specialising in different art forms, worked with a range of community groups to explore their current perceptions of libraries and what they might want in the future from their library service. Additionally a number of open arts-based consultation sessions took place to enable everyone in the community to contribute to the consultation if they so wished. This activity was supplemented by a series of sessions facilitated by North West Planning Aid, an organisation that specialises in empowering and involving local people in planning issues that potentially have an impact on their community. The participants in all the consultation sessions undertook an innovative range of arts-based activities that allowed them to explore and discuss a variety of concepts and ideas.

The new High Street Library opened in June 2007. As a result of the consultation, the new library shares the premises with a number of allied services. It incorporates a one-to-one interview room and community rooms, as requested by the local community, which will be used to provide Youth Service facilities and a study support centre. This is particularly important as over 50 per cent of users at this library are aged under 16. The library is working with the Youth Service in the development of Britain's first branded Headspace,[4] where young people will be actively involved in the development and promotion of library services and reading to this age group (Bolton Council, 2006a).

Examples of participation

One form of participation might be to include members of the user community on the library board or other decision-making groups. There are also examples of users being involved in stock selection. Members of the community might also become involved in the running of the library, for example by acting as volunteer homework tutors. In Newcastle-under-Lyme in Staffordshire, for example, the one-stop shop is run by volunteers accredited by Age Concern and the Council for Voluntary Services. Using volunteers in a joint-use library can be problematic, however. Ironically, the use of student librarians, a practice common in many school libraries, is sometimes made more difficult in a joint-use school-public library.

Communities and joint-use libraries in developing countries

It is not only the developed world where joint-use libraries have a role to play in promoting community cohesion. Discussing libraries in Africa, Kempson (1986) argued that community information services should be rooted in the community and, for the most part, facilitated by members of that community. Alemna (1995) advocates the model of a community information centre which provides reading material and advice to local citizens, supported by the local community financially and administratively. Mostert (1998) argues that community libraries, when established by the communities themselves, might be more successful in rural Africa than traditional public libraries which are more geared towards a literate middle class. Another key factor in the success of a community library is having library staff with local knowledge.

Social capital at Mount Barker community library, South Australia

One of the most interesting studies of the role of a joint-use library in promoting social inclusion and encouraging community cohesion is the social capital audit carried out at Mount Barker joint-use college-public library; this was conducted in 2004 and described by Candy Hillenbrand (2005). Social capital is defined as 'the processes between people which establish networks, norms, social trust and facilitate co-ordination and co-operation for mutual benefit'.

The survey showed that, for many users, the library fulfilled a social role in addition to the traditional function of lending books. Young people were the most sociable of all the groups using the library: they saw it as a safe place and somewhere to hang out and meet friends. People over 60 were also a sociable group, with many talking to acquaintances, strangers and library staff. When people were asked to describe the benefits of the library, equality of access for all was the second most highly ranked theme, followed by the library as a place, social interaction and the community role of the library. People valued the fact that the library gave them access to materials they would not normally be able to afford. They saw it as a peaceful, relaxing space and a safe haven that is open and welcoming to all. The library was thought to have a role in bringing families together, creating a sense of community and providing a focal point. This is supported by the library's management and vision, which have shifted significantly in recent years; two of the four strategic drivers are now social inclusion and community partnerships. As part of a strategy aimed at addressing the issue of social exclusion of young people, a youth officer has been appointed and plans to involve young people actively in the selection process. There are also plans to change the library's policy on temporary residents (this required them to pay a deposit to join the library), and to reduce fines.

Conclusions

Due to their need to serve more than a single, homogeneous user group, joint-use libraries, perhaps more than any other type of library, need to be aware of the needs of their communities. Many joint-use libraries are making real efforts to provide services and facilities which can help to combat social exclusion and increase community cohesion. Key to this is working with partners, whether these are other library services or other information or service providers from the public and voluntary sectors in particular. By collaborating with those with expertise in working with particular groups, such as people with disabilities, ethnic minority groups and young people, joint-use libraries can improve the way in which they offer support to these groups to provide a more inclusive service. This approach is one that libraries from all sectors could benefit from studying more closely.

Notes

1. See The Network (2006) for examples of work in this area and further background information.
2. The report commissioned after the race riots in Bradford, Oldham and Burnley in 2001.
3. See www.peoplesnetwork.gov.uk/.
4. Further details can be found at www.readingagency.org.uk/young/ headspace/.

7

Expanding horizons

Joint-use libraries have the potential to expand horizons in many ways. They bring library services, literacy development and access to the global information network to many isolated communities which would not otherwise have access to such resources. Users of joint-use libraries, whether based in rural villages in the developing world or urban communities in more developed countries, benefit from an increased range of services and resources. For example, public library users might gain access to academic databases and other resources to allow them to carry out more in-depth research, or school pupils might enjoy a wider range of reading materials to help them to develop as confident readers through access to public library stock. Beyond these immediate benefits, joint-use libraries can alter users' perceptions of their parent organisations. A benefit cited by a number of joint-use university-public and college-public libraries is that they can help to break down barriers to university or college education among some members of the local community. Those who may not have considered studying at a college or university, or would not feel comfortable entering a formal educational establishment, may come to see the benefits of studying through using a joint-use library as a member of the public.

One example is Rockingham Regional Campus Community Library in Australia, where the joint use library has broken down barriers to university education for many local people. The city is one which, traditionally, has not valued tertiary education, but by locating the public library on the campus it has made people realise that it is not as threatening as first thought (Hamblin, 2007). In Gotland in Sweden, the area serviced by Almedalsbiblioteket, a joint university-public library, the population has little academic education. Universities are often not well understood and are looked on as closed to the public. The library therefore acts as a window to show what the academies are doing, to gain goodwill and interest from the local municipality and population and thus stimulate interest in academic studies among the population (Svensson et al., 2007). Many joint-use libraries have developed programmes specifically to support this. Metropolitan State University in Minnesota, for example, has various initiatives to encourage students from local schools to become more familiar with the university, including College for Kids, where classes of fourth- to sixth-grade students spend a day at the library and the university, and Teens Know Best, a programme involving high school students in the review of new young-adult books, facilitated by a university associate professor/librarian (Barton et al., 2007). Others have adopted a more informal approach. At The Bridge in Glasgow, UK, library staff help users to make the transition from informal to formal learning by introducing them to college tutors, thus easing the initial contact and making users feel more comfortable meeting college staff.

Furthermore, if they are co-located with other cultural and leisure services, joint-use libraries may encourage users to try new services which they may not have previously considered, such as visiting a museum or art gallery, going to the theatre or a concert, or taking part in new sports and leisure activities. A good example of a joint-use facility which brings together many of these elements is Ardnamurchan Library in the Scottish Highlands, which serves the whole of the 50 square miles (130 square kilometres) Ardnamurchan peninsula. Ardnamurchan Library is a joint-use school-community library which is part of the Sunart Centre (Arainn Shuaineirt). Facilities offered include:

- an outdoor games area;
- a games hall for badminton, basketball, football, tennis etc.;
- a fitness suite equipped with rowing, running and exercise machines, weights, multigym etc.;
- an arts venue for concerts, theatre productions, exhibitions and films;
- an adult learning centre from which Lochaber College offers a range of courses, includes videoconferencing facilities (McNicol, 2003).

Another example is The Bridge in the Easterhouse area of Glasgow, which incorporates a 250-seat arts centre, leisure and sports facilities, including a swimming pool, a dance studio, a café and recording studio facilities as well as a joint-use college-public library.

Of course, just as other cultural and leisure providers can benefit from co-locating with a library, so the library is likely to gain additional users from those visiting the complex to use other facilities. By co-locating with services outside the education and cultural sectors, joint-use libraries can expand their user base still further. Many of the groups which libraries traditionally find hard to reach, such as the economically disadvantaged, migrants and young people, can be attracted to the library when they visit to use other services such as a one-stop shop or youth centre. Co-locating with these types of services can help to alter the perceptions of libraries held by current non-users and offer them access to the wide range of resources and services that libraries provide.

This chapter will focus on one of the most significant ways in which joint-use libraries can expand horizons: through involvement in lifelong learning.

Lifelong learning

Lifelong education covers 'formal, non-formal and informal patterns of learning throughout the life cycle of an individual for the conscious and continuous enhancement of the quality of life, his own and that of society' (Dave, 1976). The adult education expert Malcolm Knowles (1990) claimed that the growth of knowledge means that people now need to learn in different ways and that learning must be an experiential, lifelong process. Recent changes in learning which are particularly relevant to libraries are:

- a greater emphasis on learning as a lifelong process;
- student- rather than teacher-centred learning;
- the use of the term 'learning' rather than education;
- a change in the role of the teacher, from a source of knowledge to a communicator or facilitator; teachers as technicians rather than authorities (Jarvis et al., 1998: 22–3).

The role which libraries from all sectors play in supporting both formal and informal learning has been recognised for a number of years, but as a consequence of the developments listed above, their importance as lifelong learning providers has been more widely recognised since 1990.

Libraries and lifelong learning policy agendas

The links between libraries and lifelong learning have been affirmed in regional, national and international policy statements for a number of years. The IFLA/UNESCO public library manifesto (1994) states: 'The public library, the local gateway to knowledge, provides a basic condition for lifelong learning, independent decision-making and cultural development of the individual and social groups.' And the *IFLA/UNESCO School Library Manifesto* (1999) says: 'The school library equips students with lifelong learning skills and develops the imagination, enabling them to live as responsible citizens.'

EBLIDA (the European Bureau of Library, Information and Documentation Associations) adopted a statement on the role of libraries in lifelong learning in 2001. The statement focuses on libraries' role in giving access to information and the librarian's role in providing expert guidance in identifying and evaluating quality resources, thus enabling users to maximise their use of the new global networks where information often lacks the traditional benchmarks of quality, authenticity and permanence.

To give an example from another part of the world, the Australian Library and Information Association believes that:

> Libraries are lifelong learning centres with education as an essential part of their mission and should acknowledge their responsibility for supporting and supplementing education within their communities, in a variety of formal and informal as well as cultural contexts. (Schamber, 1990)

Tellingly, the 2003 strategy document produced by the UK Department for Culture, Media and Sport (DCMS),

Framework for the Future, was subtitled *Libraries, Learning and Information in the Next Decade*. This set out a wide role for libraries in relation to learning.

- Libraries provide an unthreatening environment for self-motivated learning, in which people can pursue their hobbies and interests without necessarily engaging in formal courses. Libraries promote learning as exploration and self-development.

- Libraries are one of the few places where young and old, schoolchildren, college students and adult learners can all participate in learning.

- Libraries allow informal, individual learning and clubs and communities for learning, as well as providing a range of short evening and daytime courses.

- Libraries are 'learning start-up' organisations: they should excel at helping people get started with learning, whether they are children or adults returning to learning. Libraries should provide the foundations for a learning culture.

In 2004 the Museums, Libraries and Archives Council launched *Inspiring Learning for All*, 'a national framework to help all museums, libraries and archives in the process of transformation into accessible and dynamic learning organisations'. A key element of the framework is the development of generic learning outcomes to evaluate the impact of all activities undertaken by learning organisations. There are five defined outcomes:

- knowledge and understanding;
- skills;
- attitudes and values;

- enjoyment, inspiration and creativity;
- activity, behaviour and progression.

Of course, it is not just public libraries that wish to measure the impact they have on learning. This is, perhaps, even more important for libraries based within an educational institution, which will be concerned with supporting both formal and informal learning. For example, the English school library self-evaluation framework focuses on evaluating school libraries' contribution to learning and teaching (Department for Education and Skills, 2004c). The 'evalued' toolkit for university and college libraries (Evidence Base, 2006) includes sections on evaluating the impact of electronic information services on learning, teaching, graduate skills and research. As it says:

> In order to avoid being marginalised in the increasingly learner-focused environment of higher education institutions, library services need to respond positively to the new learning agenda. With the shifting emphasis from teacher-led instruction to independent student learning, library staff are required to play a more significant role in learner support. The development and increasing prevalence of blended learning, e-learning and other new methods of course delivery are central to any evaluation of the impact of EIS (Electronic Information Services) on learning and teaching. It is essential that libraries and EIS are seen as an integral part of learning and teaching, rather than an add-on, as students are increasingly likely to expect access to a range of EIS resources and services as a fundamental part of their course.

The role of joint-use libraries in lifelong learning

Joint-use libraries, especially those which include a formal learning provider such as a school or university together with a public library, have the potential to act as a bridge been formal and informal learning, combining elements of both types of providers to give a more holistic learning experience for users.

This has been explicitly stated as one of the main objectives for some joint-use libraries, perhaps no more so than in the case of the Dr Martin Luther King Jr Library in San José, where the potential impact of the arrangement has been described by the university library dean, Patricia Breivik, as follows:

> When you come in from the city side and look through the atrium, you see the campus. What that's saying to families where no one's gone to college is: You can get a college education that's only one step beyond your public library. To me, that is architecturally the most important message this building gives out. (Quoted in Jordan, 2005: 49)

The vision of this joint-use library has three main elements which emphasise the significance of education and learning: to enrich lives with lifelong learning and access to ideas and information; to provide students, instructors and community with access to information needed for education and personal growth; and to support San José State University's educational mission in expanding the base of knowledge through research and scholarship (SJLibrary.org, 2007a).

Ruth Kifer (2007) describes how, because of the combined resources of the two library organisations and the ability to integrate services in one facility, lifelong learning opportunities have become available for the entire community, whether someone is formally enrolled in an educational programme or not. Students in classroom groups receive instruction in the use of digital databases; community groups mount displays in the exhibit area; children attend story hours; community members lead tours of the facility; and faculty members consult with librarians regarding their research projects. The library's Educational Resource Center facilitates outreach to the educational community, including schools, teachers, students in the university's educational programme and teaching faculty in the College of Education. A culture of reading is promoted throughout the university and the community. The library is a co-sponsor of the community reading programme, Silicon Valley Reads, and also co-sponsors the Campus Reading Program each year. The university's Center for Literary Arts brings numerous well-known authors to the campus for events, which quite often are held in the library. It is also interesting to note that the web portals which provide entry points to the library's online resources for users are described as 'learning pathways'.

School-public joint-use libraries

Research in the USA, especially the Colorado studies, has established links between student achievement and certain characteristics of school libraries, namely library media (LM) programme development, information technology, teacher/library media specialist (LMS) collaboration and individual visits to the library media centre (LMC). In addition, as participation increases in leadership roles, so does collaboration between teachers and LMSs. The relationship between these factors and Colorado Student Assessment Program (CSAP) reading scores is not explained away by other school or community conditions. This research highlights the fact that there are links between students' test scores and:

- LMS hours per 100 students;
- total staff hours per 100 students;
- print volumes per student;
- periodical subscriptions per 100 students;
- electronic reference titles per 100 students;
- LM expenditures per student;
- numbers of computers enabling teachers and students to utilise LMC resources, either within the LMC or networked to the LMC, licensed databases and the internet;
- LMSs spending more time planning cooperatively with teachers, identifying materials for teachers, teaching information literacy skills to students, providing in-service training to teachers and managing a computer network through which the LM programme reaches beyond its own walls to classrooms, labs and offices;
- students choosing to visit the LMC as individuals, separate from a class visit (Lance et al., 2002).

If these are the key factors in raising student achievement in a school library, a joint-use school-public library can clearly offer a number of advantages, including longer opening hours, more opportunities for students to use the library individually, more skilled staff, access to a wider range of resources (printed and electronic) and more networked computers.

Linking formal and informal learning

As previously stated, those joint-use libraries which involve partners from both formal and informal learning or education providers can help to create links between the two sectors. This means that skills and knowledge of staff specialising in each can be shared and, more importantly, the divisions between the two become less apparent from a user's perspective. While it is important not to assume that moving from informal to formal learning is a natural and desired route for all learners, it is likely that many will chose to move from informal study at the library to a more formal course if the two services are combined.

A good example of the way in which formal and informal learning providers complement each other within a joint-use facility is the Alvin Sherman Library in Florida. This library has 14 electronic classrooms, many of which are used for teaching as well as demonstrating new databases and other products to staff and faculty. Others can be used by community members to demonstrate new software products or for videoconferencing. One e-classroom is devoted to youth and is set up to teach simple programs to children. E-classrooms have also supported the summer computer camp for adults. The library building is wireless, as is the entire campus, and laptops are available for checkout in the library. Regular events for youth and families include a bilingual story time; the Family Literacy University that brings together pre-schoolers and their carers and aims to encourage a lifetime of reading; a summer reading programme that encourages children to read during the summer break; and other programmes related to subjects of interest to children and families in the local community (MacDougall, 2007).

Learning centres

Learning centres are an increasingly common model of joint-use provision linking formal and informal learning providers. They usually involve a public library service and an adult learning, or 'skills for life', provider. Although these do not strictly fit within the definition of joint use employed throughout this book, they are considered here because of their importance in relation to lifelong learning and their increasing prevalence. Indeed, there is no reason why almost any joint-use library which has a public, college or university element should not partner with an adult learning provider to offer a learning centre experience for users. As the research report 'Public libraries: supporting the learning process' (McNicol and Dalton, 2003) points out, the processes of reflection on learning, generalisation of learning, guiding learners and evaluating learning are often not well understood or supported in libraries, so partnering with organisations with greater expertise in these areas can help libraries to improve how they support learners throughout the learning process. The following case studies illustrate the different approaches that can be taken to the establishment of joint-use learning centres.

Case study: Zentrum für Information und Bildung, Germany

At the Zentrum für Information und Bildung (ZIB or Centre for Information and Education) in Unna in Westphalia, a joint-use public library and adult education centre has been created. ZIB, which was founded in 1999, offers 'information, advice, communication and experience'. It is located in a new building that contains education and training rooms, a library, computer rooms, a photo lab, a self-learning centre with PCs which have internet access and learning software, studios, a relaxation room, a dancing and movement room, a room for media art, an archive and reading room, seminar rooms and an open space for events. ZIB has a multidisciplinary staff of 38 people employed on a full-time basis. The centre was founded in the context of the federal government's 'Learning Regions – Promoting Networks' programme that consists of representatives from education, economy and administration. ZIB is at the heart of the network 'Learning and Learning Culture in Unna' and integrates both educational and cultural institutions. The centre perceives itself as an administrative office for citizens; an information market; a place that stimulates learning with all senses; and as a cultural, as well as a social, place. Most importantly, ZIB strives to establish lifelong learning in the region on a sustainable basis.

The library is on four levels:

- a library for children with an education room for families and a small stage for lectures and performances;
- a library for adolescents, with a meeting place used for leisure as well as a centre for pupils;
- a zone for specialised books;
- a fiction area.

There are 14 multimedia PCs which can be connected to the internet in the public zone of the library, and an additional 36 PCs in other areas of the complex. ZIB aims its services at local and regional citizens and there are special programmes for children and adolescents (Reading Commune Unna), artistically active people (studio and room for media art), self-learners (learning meetings), groups who are reluctant to learn, those who are illiterate and immigrants.

ZIB is an informal learning provider, but it issues certificates in computer skills and various languages, which are officially recognised. The centre is open to all, but special attention is given to groups which are not very motivated to learn or which so far have had no, or only restricted, access to education. At present ZIB reaches about 9,000 participants with its educational offer each year. The library is visited by 130,000 people annually, of whom 4,500 are active users (Buiskool et al., 2005).

Case study: Oldham Library and Lifelong Learning Centre

Oldham Library and Lifelong Learning Centre brings together children's, adult and reference libraries, as well as a performance space, ICT-intensive teaching rooms, a Skills for Life (Maths and English) Centre, art rooms and a crèche. Adjoining Gallery Oldham, it is the second phase of a new cultural quarter in the town. The design of the library is intended to make learning, art, reading and performance accessible to the whole community. It is a strong symbol of multicultural learning, integrating community facilities with the library service. Proof of its success is in the sharp rise in visitors, who more than doubled in numbers in the year following its opening in 2006. As well as meeting current needs, it provides for flexibility and expansion. It was one of the finalists in the Prime Minister's Better Public Buildings Awards 2007. The library is open seven days a week and includes specialist children's and teenage libraries, a homework centre, extensive free computer facilities and an expanded Talking Books service (Oldham Council, undated).

Case study: University of the Highlands and Islands, UK

The University of the Highlands and Islands (UHI) in Scotland has more than 100 learning centres based in a variety of community locations, including schools, leisure centres and community centres. However, many are, in fact, joint-use libraries based in public or school/college libraries. The following core services are available at all UHI library and learning resource centres:

- access to a range of books for loan and reference, plus journals and periodicals, which support the courses offered by the UHI academic partners;

- access to computers and other information and communication technologies such as videoconferencing;

- access to the internet;

- access to electronic data such as online journals and CD-ROMs (UHI Millennium Institute, undated).

This demonstrates how joint-use libraries can extend the facilities available to isolated communities and make it possible for local people to study for higher-level qualifications without leaving their community.

Supporting literacy

Although learning centres and other forms of joint-use library help to promote learning generally, particular areas where libraries can help improve skills are literacy and information literacy. Literacy support and promotion have long been identified as among the key roles of libraries, and this is supported by many policy documents. In the UK, for instance, *Framework for the Future* identifies one of the national priorities for public libraries as 'playing a major role in the encouragement of adult literacy and pre-school learning' (Department for Culture, Media and Sport, 2003). Similarly, the Australian Library and Information Association (2006) believes that 'Libraries must actively commit time and resources to coordinating literacy activities at all levels and to promote literacy among all members of their community, users and non-users alike.'

These statements have been backed up by projects and initiatives in many countries around the world intended to improve the literacy support on offer in libraries. Just a few examples include Vital Link in the UK, Buildliteracy.org in the USA and the National Summit on Libraries and Literacy – Moving Forward in Canada.

By partnering with providers of literacy tuition and other basic skills, joint-use libraries can support literacy development. One example is the Kitengesa Library in Uganda, which offers a programme of literacy instruction based on user needs that is provided free of charge by one of the librarians. A number of community members have learned to read and write, both in the local language, Luganda, and in English, thanks to the efforts of the librarian. This service is highly individualised and of great importance to participants. They are now able to make better use of library materials and, more importantly, participate in civic and community activities that have a bearing on their quality of life (Dent, 2006).

It is not just basic literacy skills which are supported in joint-use libraries: more sophisticated reading techniques can be encouraged too. One example is bibliotherapy, which is an ideal service to offer in a health-public joint-use library, combining the skills of reader development librarians from a public library and specialists from the health sector. It introduces people to alternative ways of dealing with relatively minor health problems.

Developing information literacy skills

The 2005 Alexandria Proclamation on Information Literacy and Lifelong Learning states that information literacy is a part of lifelong literacy, holding that:

- information literacy is an essential feature of lifelong literacy in any information society;
- developing habits of enquiry in everyday life and in informal education supports information literacy;
- formal education supports information literacy by including instruction and practice in all subject areas at all educational levels;
- information literacy is a part of lifelong literacy society (UNESCO, 2005).

From this definition, it is evident that joint-use libraries have an important role to play in developing information literacy skills.

Librarians in university, school and college libraries have skills in supporting the information literacy needs of their users and delivering training sessions in various aspects of information handling. In a joint-use library these skills can be used to benefit public library users too, as programmes can be adapted and offered to public users. Reference department librarians from the Alvin Sherman Library in Florida, for example, have taught information literacy classes for public and private high schools in the county and also for hospitals and community service organisations.

At Almedalsbiblioteket in Sweden, one of the aims is to facilitate the information literacy of visitors. This means that a more problem-oriented approach to reference work has been adopted. The library staff support people in finding answers to questions, working together rather than just delivering answers. A single reference desk has been replaced by four internet computers to be used in cooperation between users and staff. Information literacy is depicted as a stepladder or staircase. The idea is to make a contribution to the information skills of all citizens, from pre-school children to university staff, aiming to arouse curiosity to ask questions, engage critical thinking and enhance ability to find adequate answers (Svensson et al., 2007).

However, the information literacy support offered needs to be tailored to the varying needs of joint-use library users. Quinlan and Tuñón (2005) describe how, at the Alvin Sherman Library in Florida, campus-based students are taught how to locate articles within their programme of studies, while a distance-learning student would be guided through the process by telephone or referred to an instruction page online. Public users who are students from other educational institutions would be taught how to do their own research, while a member of the general public would be provided with selected resources.

There are additional possibilities to develop advanced information literacy services when one of the partners in a joint-use library is from a more specialised service, for example a health library. In this case they can offer training in specialist information-seeking skills to the public, and also to other library staff. Similarly, subject librarians in a university library could help to improve the skills of both users and more generalist staff in their specialist areas.

Intergenerational learning

Where joint-use libraries perhaps have the greatest potential is in fostering intergenerational learning, where users from across a wide age range come together to learn and support each other. This might include, for example, an oral history project involving pupils and older library users in a joint school-public library, or a buddying system to mentor younger children and support literacy development in a joint school-college or college-public library. At the Metropolitan State University library in Minnesota, for instance, university students and other volunteers act as homework tutors to students in the public library, and a family literacy project involved 30 university students working with public library users (Barton et al., 2007).

Case study: North Regional/BCC Library

The Friends of North Regional/BCC Library sponsor an award-winning free tutoring programme for elementary school students. Up to 50 adult volunteers tutor an equal number of children at the library in reading and maths, one on one, for an hour each week. Beyond improved academic skills, participants also benefit from quality time spent with a mentor. In cases where parents may be working in multiple jobs, and for those who may be adjusting to a new home, a Friends tutor provides extra stability. Volunteer literacy tutors also work one on one with adult students, improving their reading skills (Broward County Board of County Commissioners, undated:b).

Widening the horizons of library staff

It is important to point out that it is not just library users whose horizons can be widened by joint-use libraries; they can also change the outlook of many library staff. As mentioned in Chapter 4, many librarians spend their entire careers within a single sector. Through working in a joint-use library with staff from other sectors, and from different professional backgrounds such as education and social services, staff can be introduced to fresh ideas and, together, find new ways of working and innovative solutions to problems. Of course, joint-use libraries also expose staff to new types of users, and this can be another way in which their horizons are widened. Interestingly, staff at The Bridge in Glasgow report that members of the library staff had been encouraged to take a course at the college as a result of working at the joint-use library.

Widening horizons within the library profession

Finally, joint-use libraries have the potential to expand horizons within the library profession as a whole. By taking, combining and adapting elements from a number of different sectors, joint-use libraries can suggest new ways of working, better methods of meeting user needs and models of library provision which hold promise for the future. It is the communication with librarians from other sectors and professionals from other services which is, perhaps, the most valuable element of joint-use libraries for the future of the profession as a whole.

One example of this is the creation of a new professional role in one of the Swedish libraries involved in the VUXBIB project, which aimed to improve public library support for adult learners. This saw the introduction of a 'study librarian': a member of staff was able to concentrate on serving a specific group of users while acting alongside the rest of the library team who continued to serve all users. This made it possible to retain the traditional role of public library staff while also expanding the range of learning opportunities on offer (Zetterlund and Garden, 2007).

Conclusions

Although the concept of a joint-use library does offer tremendous potential to support the development of lifelong learning, there are a number of difficulties which need to be overcome. Many of these have already been described in Chapter 5 – for example the communication problems which can result when two groups of professionals come together in a partnership. A particular concern for many is the difference in ethos between formal and informal learning providers. For instance, while formal providers need to track learners and are keen to improve learners' results and pass rates, these processes can be highly off-putting to informal learners. In general, informal providers, such as public libraries, have a more holistic approach to learning, focused on exploration and self-development. Furthermore, as Zetterlund and Garden (2007) point out, public and educational libraries differ in their reasoning and outlook: while academic libraries focus on solving specific educational questions, public libraries have a broader approach to learning and focus on creating a learning environment which is suitable for a wide cross-section of people. This means that tools and methods developed to support learning in the education sector may not always be suitable for a public library, or indeed a joint-use library. Whether a joint-use library is less able to support the public library's mission of offering an environment conducive to informal learning if it also supports formal educational requirements is a question in need of further investigation. However, as Ruth Kifer (2007) points out, although historically academic librarians have placed a high value on conservation, preservation, scholarship and cultural heritage, there has been a shift in emphasis in recent years and accessibility, information literacy and lifelong learning are now seen as equally important aspects of the core mission of academic libraries too.

The appropriateness of a joint-use library may in part depend on the style of learning, or learning theory, advocated by the partner organisations. For example, a university or college which supports a social learning model may be more open to the possibilities offered by a joint library. Social learning theory focuses on the learning that occurs within a social context; it considers that people learn from one another. A joint-use library brings an expansion in the possibilities for interactions between different groups, supporting the notion of the development of a learning community of practice and the integration of learning in daily life:

> ...learning is in the relationships between people. Learning is in the conditions that bring people together and organise a point of contact that allows for particular pieces of information to take on a relevance; without the points of contact, without the system of relevancies, there is not learning, and there is little memory. Learning does not belong to individual persons, but to the various conversations of which they are a part. (Murphy, 1999: 17)

A joint-use library can provide such a 'point of contact' to bring people together and stimulate learning.

8

How good are joint-use libraries? (And how do we know?)

If joint-use libraries are to be considered as a possible model for future library services, we need to be sure that they work. Informal comments from many staff working in such libraries suggest they can and do work, by providing users with better standards of service and access to a wider range of resources as well as offering a stimulating working environment for staff. However, there is little robust evidence to help convince those outside the sector of the potential benefits. Evaluation of joint-use libraries has been limited and, when it does take place, the data are not usually collated to provide a meaningful picture of the effectiveness and impact of joint-use facilities regionally, nationally or internationally.

Of course, like all libraries, joint-use libraries should be regularly evaluated to find out how well they are serving their users, identify areas for improvement, help to plan new developments and provide management information. This point has been well rehearsed in the literature of joint-use libraries. As Haycock (1979: 52) has said, 'Good management practice means constant evaluation on a formal and informal basis from both perspectives.' However, very few joint-use libraries are continuously evaluated, maybe due to lack of forethought, complacency about outcomes, discontinuous leadership or lack of staff time. Nor are many subject to any form of external review. As a consequence, difficulties in a joint-use library can remain hidden until it is too late (Bundy and Amey, 2006).

In 2006 Alan Bundy and Larry Amey published an article entitled 'Libraries like no others: evaluating the performance and progress of joint use libraries', pointing out that evaluation can help to:

- improve performance and progress of the joint-use library;

- identify and draw awareness to issues and concerns before any become critical;

- act to raise the consciousness of library staff, and others associated with the library, about its objectives and provide a valuable opportunity for reflection;

- ensure that the synergistic advantages of a joint-use library – that the whole is greater than the sum of the parts – are realised as much as possible.

The first three points apply to all types of library, although they are likely to be more complex for joint-use libraries. However, it is the final point, examining the unique 'joint-use' nature of the library, where most work needs to be done.

Existing joint-use library evaluation models

Bundy and Amey (2006) advocate three strands of evaluation for joint-use libraries:

- ongoing formative evaluation;

- an external review of the library at the end of its first three years, focused on quantitative and qualitative output measures;

- after the first external review, a cycle of external reviews every five to seven years, again focused on quantitative and qualitative output measures.

In the early 1980s South Australia's unique system of politically mandated school-community libraries provided an opportunity for Amey (1984) to develop and test an evaluation plan for those libraries. That plan remains the only known framework for joint-use library evaluation, and it was revised by Bundy and Amey in 2006. This revised plan states that the following are necessary for a joint-use library assessment.

- *Continuity*. Rather than one-off or infrequent evaluation, a method that provides an ongoing assessment of the performance and progress of the library should be used.

- *Versatility*. An assessment plan must therefore acknowledge the social, political and economic situation in which the joint-use library is operating. Such an approach should allow a meaningful assessment in a way that is not possible using a simple comparison with a general set or sets of standards.

- *Flexibility*. Any evaluative approach needs to be adaptable enough for use with different types of joint-use facilities, ranging from a library staffed by many professionals and situated in a large, multipurpose community centre to a small library managed by one professional in a rural school.

- *Practicability*. An evaluative process must be practical and feasible. The time, staffing and economic commitment required for the kind of evaluation sometimes envisioned by researchers may simply not be available.

In their article, Bundy and Amey (2006) go on to describe how the assessment plan should proceed in five steps. Their method is summarised below.

Step 1: setting goals

The goals of the school library

The facilitator separately interviews the teacher-librarian, the school principal and the chairperson of the local board of management. In each case the facilitator encourages the interviewee to identify and list the school library's most important goals for the coming year.

The goals of the public library

After the goals for the school library are identified, the facilitator repeats the process for the public library, asking the participants individually about what they see as the most important goals for the library's operation as a public library. These are listed on a priority basis.

Step 2: identifying critical success factors

The critical success factors (CSFs) are those areas in which the library must perform well in order to ensure it reaches its goals. The facilitator interviews each of the participants to obtain their perceptions of the CSFs underlying each of their goals.

The CSFs of the school library

Alongside the list of goals developed, a list is made of what each interviewee sees as the critical factors influencing the attainment of each goal for the school library. Once the parallel list of goals and CSFs is completed, this is reviewed, preferably in consultation with the teachers and library assistants. It may be possible to combine, eliminate or restate goals and CSFs at this stage.

The CSFs of the public library

The above procedure is repeated, with the facilitator leading each of the participants to consider those factors most relevant to the public library's success.

Step 3: establishing corporate goals and CSFs

Having considered the institution in its separate aspects, as a school library and as a public library, the participants are then asked to look at the broader corporate concerns of the joint-use library. The facilitator therefore arranges a group session in which the teacher-librarian and the community representative work together to isolate those goals that are seen as most important for the school-community library as a whole. These are listed by priority. They may repeat or resemble the lists of goals identified for the school library and the public library, but it is possible that particular school or public library goals, although important in their own right, will not make the shortlist of the most important goals for the school-community library.

Next to the list of goals is recorded what the group feels are the CSFs underlying the attainment of the goals. Once again the list is discussed and reviewed.

Step 4: developing an action plan

At this point there should be a clear picture of the joint-use library's goals and CSFs. The next step is a plan of action, which should draw upon the strength of the whole group, with all participants contributing ideas and suggestions on how to meet the CSFs.

Step 5: designing measures of success

To assess the effectiveness of the action plan, measures of success are needed. The measures needed, and how they will be collected, should be decided before the action plan is implemented. In this way, measures can be tailored to provide the information required.

It is argued that the CSF method encourages a reappraisal of where the library is headed and where it can be improved. It also brings together the participants and requires them to share perceptions of the joint-use library's role, objectives and improvement (Bundy and Amey, 2006).

Examples of evaluation in practice

Many joint-use library practitioners cite increased usage and higher issue figures compared to a previous library or comparable stand-alone library as evidence of success. It is true that this does indicate user acceptance, and is one aspect of the value of the service. However, such measures are not sufficient on their own. Unfortunately, the few in-depth evaluations of joint-use libraries reported in the literature have almost invariably been single efforts, carried out once and never repeated; they have thus been of limited practical use in the overall development and improvement of the library or in the advancement of knowledge across the sector. Sadly, although Amey's methodology was used in a number of South Australian school-community libraries in the 1980s, in a survey in 2007 it was not being used in any (Bundy, 2007).

The following are some of the few practical examples of more well-considered evaluation activities which have been tried in different types of joint-use library.

Case study: Dr Martin Luther King Jr Library, San José

Berger's (2000) *Public and School Libraries: Issues and Options of Joint Use Facilities and Cooperative Use Agreements* is one of the few guideline documents to acknowledge that the starting point for evaluation should be during the initial planning of the joint-use library, not as an afterthought once it is operating and perhaps starting to experience tensions and difficulties. It advocates:

> Assessing the success of the combined library requires comparing before and after information. This includes cost, usage and survey information. While still in the planning stage of creating the library, information should be assembled which can be used after the combined library is in operation. This includes circulation figures for both libraries, program attendance, library visits, and operating costs. A before and after community survey can tell much about the success of the operation and about if premerger assumptions were valid. (Berger, 2000: 17)

San José's Dr Martin Luther King Jr Library commenced the collection of public and university library data two years ahead of the opening of the joint library. Surveys were conducted to measure the satisfaction level of library users prior to the merger, and then twice after it took place.

The library has also worked with the Business and Psychology Faculty at San José State University to study library staff response to working in a merged environment. It is now moving towards a new approach to evaluation and assessment to reflect a more user-centric philosophy of service (Kifer, 2007).

Case study: Blackburn Connected

Blackburn Connected in West Lothian, Scotland, is an integrated service with generic staff delivering all customer service centre and library services from one location and at first point of contact. The partnership is assessed employing the West Lothian Assessment Model,[1] the Charter Mark[2] and the PLQIM (Public Library Quality Improvement Matrix).[3] The results will be used to shape future service delivery in Blackburn and beyond. The aim is to set precise, measurable and meaningful standards for the core business of the service, which reflect the needs, expectations and rights of customers. The service will be measured against these standards, which include mandatory standards such as those set out by the Audit Commission, processing times, accuracy rates, service outputs and quality of provision. Customers will be involved in setting and monitoring standards and reporting on the findings (Brough, 2007).

The difficulty of evaluating joint-use libraries

Evaluation within the library sector as a whole is often weak, but why are joint-use libraries, in particular, so difficult to evaluate?

A lack of common aims

One possible reason is that many joint-use libraries lack a formal agreement which sets out the aims of the library. Indeed, it is difficult to find recorded examples of discussion between the partner organisations about the aims of a joint-use library. In many cases it seems that, to a large extent, each of the management bodies retains its own aims (e.g. public library service aims or school aims). Although this helps to ensure that the level of service provided to each community of users is maintained, it does not allow for the evaluation and monitoring of more collaborative aims which should be part of the mission of a shared facility.

The difficulty of evaluating partnership elements

In most cases a method can be found to evaluate the discrete elements of a joint-use library (e.g. school library provision, public library provision) in isolation. What is more difficult, however, is to evaluate the effectiveness of the collaboration and the way in which a joint-use library is 'more than the sum of the parts'.

One way to do this may be to adapt partnership evaluation methodologies used in other sectors. In the UK, for example, the Department for Communities and Local Government's Neighbourhood Renewal Unit has devised a performance management framework.[4]

Another example is the Suffolk Partnership Evaluation Toolkit[5] developed by Suffolk County Council, UK. This self-assessment inventory is based on the following principles.

Action focus

- Does the partnership have a clear, agreed, long term vision of what it wants to achieve?

- Does the partnership have a shared set of values to which all members subscribe?

- Does the partnership add value to the sphere of work it is contributing to and ensure that it is not working in isolation?

- Does the partnership use feedback from the local community to identify needs?

- Does the partnership encourage innovation and improve processes?

- Does the partnership have a positive impact on the way services are delivered?

Efficiency

- Have available resources been matched against the partnership's plans?

- Given its objectives, does the partnership have the right balance between strategic and operational activities?

- Do partnership members reflect the views of the membership of the organisations they represent?

- Does the partnership have effective support and administration arrangements?

- Are meetings effective and timetabled, with arrangements in place for communications between meetings?

- Has consideration been given to the lifetime of the partnership and whether it should continue? Is this reviewed regularly?

Inclusivity

- Does the partnership ensure that its membership reflects the purpose of the partnership?

- Does the partnership ensure that all the partners have the capacity to be fully engaged in the partnership?

- Is the management and chairing of the partnership able to provide an inclusive and impartial overview?
- Does the partnership work democratically and is it accountable to stakeholders?
- Are the partnership's decisions open to scrutiny? E.g. open meetings, minutes recorded and publicly available?

Learning and development

- Does the partnership learn from and disseminate best practice?
- Is appropriate use made of the wide range of skills and expertise of partnership members?
- Does the partnership learn from stakeholders and apply this to service improvement?
- Does the partnership find out why members leave or fail to engage with the partnership, and learn lessons for the future?
- Is the partnership able to adapt to a changing environment?

Performance management

- Does the performance management process include clear milestones, outcomes, indicators and delivery dates?
- Is the financial position monitored and reported regularly to the partnership?
- Do partners deliver what they have signed up to do?
- Are partners' resources (including buildings and staff) effectively used to meet the aims of the partnership?
- Do partners share information to support planning and management?

This would seem to be a useful tool as a basis for the evaluation of the joint-use library as a partnership.

Lack of knowledge of customer-focused evaluation methods

In the past, the library sector as a whole has largely shied away from more customer-focused forms of evaluation, preferring to judge performance based on statistics – often crude input/output measures. However, in a joint-use library, perhaps more than any other, users or customers are central to the success or otherwise of the library. It is the nature of its user groups that makes each joint-use library different from other types of library and unique in its own right. It is therefore critical that users are regularly consulted, and hopefully actively involved, in the development of the library. In doing this, it is important to ensure that the full range of users are involved and the demands of one group do not come to dominate, leaving other users sidelined.

Library standards

Standards form an important aspect of library evaluation. According to Patricia McNamee:

> Standards may be defined as a degree or level of requirement, excellence or attainment that serve as a point of reference for comparison and evaluation. They are a framework for planning and achieving best practice and excellence in the management and provision of library services. At the same time, standards provide a baseline measurement for providing an essential, or basic, level of service. (Committee on Public Libraries Housed in Schools, 2006: 34)

For the most part, standards for joint-use libraries *per se* do not exist. Bundy and Amey (2006) argue that the uniqueness of most joint-use situations militates against the creation of standards and general evaluation criteria for them. Variation among joint-use libraries in such fundamental areas as clientele, siting, size, staffing, administration and funding make the application of a single set of evaluative criteria extremely problematic. By their nature, joint-use libraries are often innovative in development and individual in their response to a particular situation. They therefore also resist meaningful benchmarking against other libraries. However, there are some examples of benchmarking between similar joint-use libraries. For instance, Deb Hamblin (2007) reports that a number of other organisations use Rockingham Regional Campus Community Library in Australia as a benchmark and the library staff spend considerable time assisting others to see both the positive and negative aspects of a joint-use facility. The library is recognised as best practice internationally by an Australian government report into the effectiveness of community partnership (Shoemaker et al., 2000).

A few examples of standards specifically for joint-use libraries do exist. One is the 'School/public library joint use facility standards' developed by the New Jersey Association of School Librarians, New Jersey Library Association and New Jersey State Library (2003). This document is based around the main challenges facing joint-use libraries, identified as:

- ensuring the safety of children;

- differing missions and constituencies, and the impact of these on the focus of collections;

- the legal basis for different types of libraries.

From this, a checklist has been developed covering the following themes:

- governance (funding arrangements, state laws and regulations);
- planning (community involvement, process for handling disputes);
- staffing (certification requirements);
- facility (accessibility, separate entrances, parking, caretaking, signage, furniture, areas for different activities, e.g. group instruction);
- focus of the collection (cataloguing, collection development policies, policies for sharing materials);
- funding (minimum levels, joint plans for capital improvements, yearly operating budget);
- hours of opening (weekends, evenings);
- internet access (dedicated PCs for adult users, joint plan for purchase and maintenance of technology).

In Alberta in Canada, the Committee on Public Libraries Housed in Schools (2006) set out standards which are intended to:

- ensure equity in the level and delivery of services;
- act as a point of reference for self-evaluation;
- provide a rational framework for future development;
- accommodate change in policy, technology and formats of materials;
- encourage cooperation.

The minimum essential standards are recommended based on the standards for member libraries with Alberta's regional library systems (Alberta Municipal Affairs and Housing, 2003). The themes covered by these standards are:

- governance/management (duties of library board);
- facilities (space requirements, signage, entrance, parking, disabled facilities etc.);
- technology (number of workstations, internet access, security, training, performance management);
- hours of opening (number of hours based on population, and times, e.g. evenings/weekends);
- collections (number of items of each type – e.g. periodicals, books – types, weeding, collection management policy, intellectual freedom, usage statistics);
- reference and information services;
- inter-library loans;
- programmes;
- staffing (number and qualifications based on population, knowledge, training, personnel policies).

Single-sector standards

Although standards for joint-use libraries are rare, there are numerous examples of such documents for single-sector libraries – some are given in Appendix II. A difficulty for many joint-use libraries is that they are required to conform to standards for one or more sectors without allowance for their joint-use nature. Some of the implications for joint-use libraries of just a few standards are discussed below.

In the UK, joint-use libraries which have a public library element are required to conform to the Department for Culture, Media and Sport's (2006) *Public Library Service*

Standards. In fact, joint-use libraries are seen by some authorities as an effective means of helping to meet certain standards.

- PLSS1 requires local authorities to provide data on the proportion of households living within a specified distance of a static library. By providing facilities in locations where a stand-alone library would not be feasible, joint-use libraries can help some local authorities to meet the required standard.

- PLSS2 measures the aggregated scheduled opening hours per 1,000 population. Because they need to serve other user groups, joint-use libraries are often open for longer hours than equivalent branches.

- PLSS6 is the number of library visits per 1,000 population. The standards state that, where a library has other council services integrated into the space or is part of a multiservice centre, only those who use the library element of the overall provision count as library visitors. However, a joint-use library could help to increase visitor numbers as other user groups (e.g. school pupils, college students) would count as library visitors within a shared library space.

Joint-use libraries can thus offer one means of achieving the required standards for public library services. On the other hand, there can be problems in meeting certain standards in a joint-use library. For instance, one standard where joint-use provision could be problematic is PLSS10 – time taken to replenish the lending stock on open access or available on loan. In some types of library (e.g. academic, research) older stock will need to be kept on the shelves; for example, seminal texts in a subject area.

Similarly, SCONUL's (2007) statistical returns for academic libraries ask for data which could be affected by the fact that a library is a joint-use facility. For example, the number of libraries and number of study spaces may well be greater in an institution with a joint-use library than in an equivalent institution without. The numbers of users entering the library and users in the library on sample days could also be greater in a joint-use facility than they would be otherwise, as could the numbers of loans, active borrowers, enquiries handled and so forth. Depending on the staffing model adopted, the number of staff may also be greater than in a dedicated academic library.

In a joint school-public library in England, the support of the public library service could be an important aspect in several elements of a school library's self-evaluation – in particular the effectiveness of links with parents and the community (Strand 6) and the LRC's role in promoting reading for enjoyment (Strand 5a) (Department for Education and Skills, 2004c).

Joint-use libraries may thus assist libraries from various sectors to meet targets and provide a better service to users. However, at present there is usually little guidance within single-sector standards as to how joint-use libraries should be assessed. There are clearly some areas where the measures for single-sector libraries are not suitable for a joint-use facility, and there is a lack of clarity as to how certain measures should be determined accurately in a joint-use library.

Guidelines and checklists

Less formal than standards, guidelines or checklists can provide a useful starting point for an evaluation. Based on a list developed by Wisconsin's Department of Public Instruction (1998), Alan Bundy (2003) devised a checklist which could be applied to community college-public or university-public libraries as well as school-community libraries.

Planning

- Similarities and differences in the mission statements of the school library and the public library are understood and reconcilable.

- The school and public library catchment areas are similar.

- A preliminary feasibility study has been conducted.

- Relevant groups have examined the complementary roles of school and public libraries and are aware of the services, resources and access that must be offered to meet the needs of both client groups.

- Community groups are involved in, and support, the decision to have a joint-use library.

- Teachers and the student representative council are involved in, and support, the decision to have a joint-use library.

- The parties that will govern the library will define their responsibilities in a formal agreement.

- An evaluation programme will be specified in the agreement.

- Dissolution of the joint-use library will be provided for in the agreement.

- Population growth or decline projected for the catchment area has been considered.

Administration and funding

- The operation of the library has been agreed to, including the opening hours, budgeting, access to resources and activities and authority for daily decision-making.

- Collection development and access policies consistent with the mission statements have been developed for both the school and public library use.

Access to information, resources and facilities

- A policy for access for all age groups and maturity levels has been agreed.

- It is accepted that children and teachers from other public and private schools in the community may use the library.

- It is accepted that home-schooled children and their parents may use the library.

- The library will be accessible by the public at any time it is open, and through a visible public entrance.

- Censorship, internet access and filtering issues have been addressed.

- It is recognised that the group licensing of electronic products may require special negotiation and investment.

- The library provides adequate space to implement the full range of school and public library services and technology.

- The library has potential for extension.

- A process for identifying and addressing future space needs is included in the agreement.

- The need for some clients to be transported to the library is recognised.

- The possible need for the library to offer a home delivery service is recognised.

- The title of the library will make it clear who may use it.

- The importance of directional and site signage is recognised.

- Furniture, furnishings and ambience are as non-institutional as possible.
- Public washrooms are available in the library or adjacent to it.
- A community meeting room is available.
- Provision is made for people with disabilities.

Attitudinal factors

- Decision-makers, administrators and employees are genuinely enthusiastic about the project and dedicated to making it work.
- Improving facilities, service, resources and access – not saving money – is the primary motivation in developing the library.
- Adults feel comfortable and welcome in the school and are accustomed to using it for public functions.
- The mixing of pre-schoolers, children, teenagers and young and older adults is not seen as threatening or uncomfortable by any of the potential users or the library's partners.
- All security and duty-of-care issues have been considered and reconciled.

In addition, a number of professional associations have provided statements of guidance for joint-use libraries within countries or regions.

The Australian Library and Information Association (2002) 'supports the establishment of joint use libraries if they equal or better the level of service which would be given in separate facilities'. It states that successful joint-use library development requires:

- the unequivocal commitment of all interested parties;
- full consultation involving all the parties concerned prior to any decision on establishment;

- professional advice at an early stage of consideration of a joint-use library;
- careful consideration of the site of the institution, and of the position and visibility of the library so that convenient access for all potential users is guaranteed;
- access by all users during the institution's operating hours, with adequate provision for use outside those hours and during vacations;
- signing of a formal agreement by each of the parties covering all areas relating to the development, funding and continued maintenance of the library;
- the size of the library and its staffing to meet the needs of the whole community served;
- formal agreement on the process to be followed for a new building or extensions if, after a period of operation, the size of the library proves to be inadequate;
- a board of management, representative of all parties and advisory to the library manager;
- an integrated staffing structure with a single library manager; where a joint-use library is to serve as the library for an educational institution and the public, the appointment of staff with education and public library expertise is desirable;
- a regular, preferably externally facilitated, evaluation of the library.

In the UK the School Library Association (2007) believes that joint/dual-use libraries work best when the school managers and the managers of the community library service have a shared vision for the facility and a clear agreement as to its operation. A vision statement might be expected to include the intention to maximise the opportunities offered to provide an inclusive service to the whole community, throughout and beyond the school day; to provide access for learners of all ages and abilities; and to promote lifelong learning and reading for pleasure. If the library is to be effective it is essential that funding is adequate to provide an appropriate level of staffing and the range and quantity of resources required to support the school curriculum and the learning needs and leisure interests of the community as a whole. An agreement on the operation of the service may take the form of a policy or a formal service-level agreement. It should include statements relating to the following aspects.

- *Access*. Ideally the library should be available to pupils throughout the school day. To maximise the advantages of being dual use, it should also be available to other members of the community during the school day and at other times (evenings and weekends) according to community needs.

- *Security*. The security of pupils will need to be considered. Staffing levels should be adequate to provide supervision and guard against inappropriate contact with members of the community, and staff should be given child protection training. The layout of the library should be designed to give good lines of sight.

- *Staffing*. There should be sufficient professional librarians and library assistants to manage the library; support the learning and personal reading needs of pupils, school staff and other members of the community; collaborate with teaching staff to support library-based learning and develop information literacy skills; and operate the library on a day-to-day basis. Line management of staff should be clearly defined.

- *Stock.* Stock should reflect both the curricular needs of the school and the needs of the local community. Ideally the stock will be integrated, but with provision for items to be retained for school use only when needed for curricular work.

- *Budget.* The budget may be held by the school or by the public library service. Ideally both should contribute an agreed proportion of it.

- *Management.* Public library and school managers should both have an input into the management of the library, but responsibilities should be clearly defined, particularly for the management of staff and of the building, so that decisions can be made quickly when necessary.

Conclusions

A number of checklists and guidelines for joint-use libraries do exist, and in general they agree on many overall principles – for example, the importance of a written agreement, the need for commitment from all partners and adequate access arrangements and staffing provision. The success factors for joint-use libraries are well known and documented. Although most guidelines have been developed with school-public libraries in mind, much of the advice they contain applies equally to other types of joint-use library. However, these guidelines have rarely been formalised into standards. This is partly due to the relatively small number of joint-use libraries in comparison to other types of libraries, but also due to the diversity between joint-use libraries themselves, which makes a single, rigid set of standards impracticable and inappropriate.

However, this does not mean that it is unrealistic to evaluate joint-use libraries; it simply means that a flexible approach needs to be taken, as described by Bundy and Amey (2006). It is in evaluating the 'corporate concerns' of joint-use libraries, to which Bundy and Amey refer, that more work needs to be done. Unless there are clear, common aims agreed on by all parties, developing an action plan and designing measures of success will be impossible. In order to evaluate the collaborative, partnership elements of joint-use libraries, library professionals may well have to look to other sectors for guidance.

All joint-use libraries need to carry out regular evaluation to ensure their individual success. However, they also need to be open about sharing this information among other joint-use librarians and within the wider library community so that others can learn from this, the evidence base can be built up and lessons about the potential for joint-use libraries communicated to those outside the sector. Although joint-use school-public libraries have been studied for several decades, in recent years a number of new models of joint-use provision have been developed. Knowledge about the success of one-stop shops, multiple partnerships and other less common forms of joint-use library is not so well developed. It is especially important that more is learnt about these newer or rarer types of joint-use library.

Notes

1. See www.mytoolkit.net/csp/WLAMlinks.pdf.
2. See www.cabinetoffice.gov.uk/chartermark/.
3. See www.slainte.org.uk/files/pdf/slic/PLQIM/plqim.pdf.
4. See www.neighbourhood.gov.uk/publications.asp?did=200.
5. See http://apps2.suffolk.gov.uk/cgi-bin/committee_xml.cgi?p=doc&id=1_4004&format=doc.

9

The future

What does the future hold for joint-use libraries? Having survived some testing times during which they have come in for criticism from policy-makers, professional bodies, researchers and other librarians, it seems that the twenty-first century may be the time when joint-use libraries finally come into their own. The examples described in this book suggest that these libraries are uniquely suited to the current political climate and drivers for change in society. They encourage collaboration and partnership working; they can be a means to promote lifelong learning, especially within communities where education has not traditionally been valued; and, perhaps most importantly of all, they can help to create a more equitable society. It is also noteworthy that many new joint-use libraries are being designed to be environmentally sustainable.[1] Of course, this is not just true of joint-use libraries, but they may have greater potential than many other types of library to contribute to sustainable public services. By gathering a raft of services under one roof, joint-use libraries and co-located services allow people in more isolated areas to access services locally rather than having to travel to a larger centre of population. Furthermore, by sharing a building, energy savings may be made.

Joint-use libraries in developing countries have not featured strongly in this book, largely because they are less well researched and publicised than those in more developed countries. The following section attempts to redress this by considering the potential of joint-use libraries in the developing world.

Joint-use libraries in developing countries

As Chapter 6 pointed out, joint-use libraries can be seen as naturally inclusive, making information resources and services available to groups who would normally be denied access to such facilities. Many joint-use libraries are actively working with their user communities to combat social exclusion and improve community cohesion. They can thus play a part in helping to create a fairer society. Nowhere is this truer than in regions of the developing world, where school-community libraries offer a cost-effective solution to the largely unmet challenge of providing free public libraries in rural areas. They are an effective means of improving and sustaining literacy, learning and access to reliable health and other information for people of all ages and circumstances. Philip (1980) set forth six objectives for rural libraries.

- To help rural children and adults maintain knowledge gained from their education.

- To help rural farmers increase productivity by providing information about such topics as soil composition, markets for different crops, dairy and poultry farming, farm mechanics, land use, preservation of soil, rainfall and cultivation of different types of crops such as coffee and tea.

- To help rural people understand the country's social, political and economic endeavours and nation-building efforts.

- To aid in the development of a wholesome family life, providing materials about family planning and healthcare.
- To provide materials to help get rid of tribalism and provincialism.
- To inspire members of the community to read, use books and enjoy these items for education and recreation.

The following examples illustrate how joint-use libraries can bring such benefits to communities in developing countries. Of course, models created in the developed world may not be appropriate for other types of community, and in each case a form of joint-use library provision needs to be found which is suited to the needs of the community in question. Although much is known about the success factors for joint-use libraries in developed countries, it cannot automatically be assumed that the same factors will apply to all areas of the world.

Case study: a rural community library in Uganda

An example of the type of joint-use library that could become more common in the future is the Kitengesa Library[2] in Uganda. Kitengesa is a rural village in south-eastern Uganda; it is a small community where until 2004 there was no running water or electricity. Masaka is the closest town, located about two miles (three kilometres) away on a dirt road. The village has several primary and secondary schools. The majority of the community members are farmers, and there are a large number of small children orphaned as result of the AIDS epidemic. Much of the population can read, as access to education has existed for quite some time in the community. In 1997 the Ugandan government instituted free universal primary education, which increased the numbers of those now able to read. Some residents can read in English, but most read in the local language of Luganda. However, access to reading materials is still minimal, and the challenge remains to providie reading materials for the newly literate.

In 1999 volunteers began to lend reading material to local school students out of a small box of 161 books. They asked students to provide some feedback on what they learned from, or enjoyed about, what they had just read. One of the goals was eventually to have a library which would be open to members of the community. In 2001 a one-room library was built on the grounds of the Kitengesa comprehensive secondary school, funded primarily by a grant from the UN One Percent for Development Fund. In 2004 another grant from this fund allowed for the purchase of solar panels to provide limited lighting in the library after sunset. The library is the only building in the village to have electricity, and users can now read during the evening hours. The long-term objectives of the Kitengesa Community Library are to promote a reading culture in Buwunga subcounty of Masaka district, Uganda, and to develop a model of a rural community library that could be replicated elsewhere.

In pursuit of these aims, the library promoters have the following short-term objectives.

- To develop a collection of books of two types: circulation books will be novels and other readers that are relatively inexpensive, and members will be allowed to borrow these books; reference books will include dictionaries, atlases, encyclopaedias and school textbooks, and members will be allowed to read these books in the library building.

- To maintain a building that has been erected for the purpose on land belonging to Kitengesa comprehensive secondary school. This building will be used for storing books and making them available for reading. It may also be used for other community purposes, such as meetings and concerts.

- To raise funds to support both the book collection and the building.

Kitengesa Community Library has a dual role as both a community library and a school library. It is intended for three target groups: staff and students of Kitengesa comprehensive secondary school; staff and students of neighbouring primary schools; and any other residents of Buwunga subcounty. The library seats about 28 users and has a collection of 1,739 books (in August 2005), as well as subscriptions to two daily newspapers. As of August 2005 there were 503 members of the library. Membership is free for students and teachers, and community members are asked to pay $1 per year in order to check out books. The library is maintained by a small staff, including two librarians and four library scholars – students who work at the library in exchange for school fees and room and board. Funding for the library comes exclusively from individual donations and grants; there is no government support provided.

The Kitengesa Community Library is unique in several ways. The collection features reading materials in both English and Luganda, and many of the Lugandan books are published by Ugandan publishers. This keeps the collection relevant and meaningful for community members. When selecting stock, every effort is made to link information directly to the needs of users. Local newspapers provide important information about the local area and the rest of the country. Publications targeting adolescents, containing articles and information about topics such as sexual health, family and relationships, are exceptionally important because of the increased rates of HIV transmission. The library has also hosted programmes aimed at women, in an attempt to provide resources for sustaining a healthy family and household. All these efforts are intended to help community members cope with issues that might arise in their daily lives. The location of the library on school grounds gives immediate access for students and teachers, but it is also conveniently located for the community to use. The library is managed by a small board of directors, which includes community members and the school's headmaster; the headmaster also serves as director of library operations.

The Kitengesa librarians are active members of the community, well known and respected, and speak both English and Luganda. They actively suggest new services, and keep track of what library users are reading and suggest new titles accordingly. Readers frequently ask for help in understanding something they have read, and the librarians provide feedback and answer questions. The librarians are also well known outside the village, and this exposure affords them some degree of status in the wider community. In addition to providing access to reading material, the librarians give literacy instruction to those in the community who seek to improve their reading and writing skills, or who wish to learn how to read and write for the first time.

Library staff work with local community leaders, including the chairman of the local branch of the National Resistance Movement, the catechist and members of the local council, to organise events that will raise awareness of the library. The library also hosts a number of regular activities. Every day during term-time a student newspaper club meets to read the newspapers to one another. Every Wednesday a women's group comes to the library to work on reading and writing and learn such skills as bookkeeping.

And every Saturday is games night, with snakes and ladders, Ludo, dominoes and Scrabble. There are monthly meetings of the Straight Talk Club, featuring a student newspaper that provides sex education and teaches students how to avoid AIDS. The students read the newspaper in single-sex groups and then boys and girls meet to discuss their responses.

Although it is intended to serve neighbouring primary schools, by August 2005 the library had only two children under ten among its members, so it initiated a campaign to bring the children in. The first step was a children's reading tent which was set up outside the library for displaying books, and ten children from each of 12 primary schools were invited, together with three teachers from each school and local dignitaries. The Reading Association of Uganda came to help with the tent and made a donation of children's books. The facilitators, together with the teachers, librarians and library scholars, organised activities for the children, including not only reading but painting, drawing, writing, singing and dancing. There were also speeches and a meal. Following the success of this event, the first Saturday of every month has been designated Children's Day. Children are invited from neighbouring primary schools, and the library scholars lead them in similar activities (Dent, 2006; Kitengesa Community Library, 2004).

Case study: community-school libraries in Zimbabwe

Twenty-three school-community libraries were established in rural Zimbabwe as part of the Rural Libraries and Resource Development Programme. These are organised and managed by local bodies such as churches, schools or community groups and have very close ties to the local community. They rely on donations rather than being supported by government funding, and use local expertise to establish and run the libraries.

Since the late 1990s the Edward Ndlovu Memorial Library has helped to fund and establish school-community libraries in Zimbabwe. It aims to promote development through community projects, improve performance of schools and pupils and promote a reading culture among pupils and teachers. It currently runs 'book box' schemes in 30 rural schools, which have an average of 300 books covering a range of subjects for ages six years to adult. These book boxes have often acted as a motivator for the setting up of permanent libraries in schools.

The response from local communities has been extremely positive. Key to the ethos of school-community libraries in Zimbabwe is that they are community-led. For example, stock is selected to meet the needs of the community. Books are donated through organisations such as Book Aid International and Books Abroad, but teachers, head-teachers and library staff are involved in the selection process to choose books which meet the needs of their community. The libraries are usually a converted classroom, with shelves and other furniture being built by members of the community. In some libraries, school leavers are encouraged and trained to staff the library under the supervision of a teacher. All the rules and regulations regarding the running of the library are determined by the community. A community worker has been engaged to work with communities on identified projects using information from books – for example, women and do-it-yourself. External support is provided by trainers from the Ministry of Education, training colleges, professional librarians, NGOs and similar agencies which offer regular training and workshops for library staff.

There are, of course, some problems. Staff turnover is high because community librarians are volunteers. The narrow publishing base in Zimbabwe is a problem, and local book distribution is poor. A number of factors present significant challenges; for instance, subsistence farming, low income, poverty, disease and government policy (Ndlovu, 2007).

Case study: Wesbank library project, South Africa

This case study illustrates some of the problems that can face newly established joint-use libraries in communities which are still developing. Wesbank is a post-apartheid township which emerged in 1999 as a reconstruction and development housing project, growing out of an informal settlement. It is a community of approximately 25,000 people, mostly former farm workers, people from other low-income areas in the Western Cape and a small Xhosa community. The area has a shop, three primary schools, one secondary school and various informal economic enterprises. However, in 2003 there was no public library or school library.

Space for a new library was secured at the newly built high school, and a library collection was started with a donated set of encyclopaedias. Further donations were received from visiting librarians, learners and tourists. During the day the library serves as a school library, while in the afternoons and evening it is open to the community, supporting the activities of the school's lifelong learning centre. Four postgraduate students from the University of the Western Cape were allocated to the project as part of their service learning training in social development, and two teachers from the school were sponsored to attend professional training at the university towards an Advanced Certificate in Education (ACE) in School Librarianship. However, it has not been possible to appoint a dedicated school librarian. A committee was established to oversee the project. The provision of refreshments became a way of attracting learners and volunteers. However, it has proved difficult to engage the community because of a lack of communal trust; social capital is still developing in the area. While the community has expressed a need for services, local people are not willing to participate in creating an effective library service. As Sally Witbooi (2006: 49) acknowledges: 'Calling for goodwill, enthusiasm, donation and time in a community experiencing economic hardship and crime became a battle of enormous will power.'

New models of joint-use library provision

Despite their long history, innovation and experimentation are still high among joint-use libraries. New models of provision are constantly being developed – for example, the major development planned in Worcester in the UK which will include not only the university and public libraries but also the County Record Office (archives), the County Archaeology Service and the City Council Customer Service Centre; or the Lower Orchards proposal in Bolton to revamp primary and special schools into integrated infant and junior sites which, if the plans go ahead, will include a local authority nursery, infant classes from special and primary schools, a children's centre, a youth centre and a relocated public library to act as the centre library (Keane, 2007).

Joacim Hansson (2007) makes a very relevant point when he suggests that, in time, users 'will enter the joint-use library wondering what the "joint use" means', because they are only aware of a single library rather than two organisations which have joined together. As he points out, the traditional division of libraries into sectors such as academic and public are representative of a specific form of social stratification and knowledge interests. Over time, the names given to joint-use libraries, their appearance and other signifiers are likely to change.

The present author would go further, to suggest that in the future the vast majority of libraries will effectively be joint-use facilities. The term may cease to be used to describe a particular type of library, but instead all libraries will incorporate some basic principles of joint-use services. More and more public libraries are becoming co-located, sharing space, staff and resources with other information providers or, indeed, providers of other types of services. Similarly, university and college libraries are making greater efforts to engage with their local communities and provide services for them, whether in the form of a full-scale joint-use library or a more limited service such as reciprocal access arrangements. For school libraries too, joint-use facilities are likely to become more and more common, especially in the UK, where they are likely to be provided as part of an extended school[3] complex. In fact, in time, if current trends continue, it is traditional stand-alone libraries which may become a rarity.

Many joint-use library staff, and other professionals working in similar environments, have commented that users do not care who provides a service; they are solely concerned with access to the resources and services which they need. However, the partners involved in some joint-use libraries are struggling to retain sight of this. Rather than focusing on their users, some become concerned with preserving their individuality and identity as an organisation and not becoming the less dominant partner. Creating a joint-use library should not just be about bringing two or more organisations together, but about creating a flexible, responsive information and learning environment which meets the needs of twenty-first-century library users. This does not necessarily mean that a fully integrated service is always the most appropriate solution; the model of joint-use provision will vary depending on local circumstances.

Good joint-use libraries are inherently user-centred; they look for the best way to provide the services that users need regardless of the organisation involved. They can be seen as post-modern organisations, in the sense that they are flexible, with unclear boundaries and collaborative internal structures, and rely on flows of information across the organisation. It could also be argued that the key features of a joint-use library are not its constituent parts, but its relationships, sense of community, partnerships and collaborations (Ray, 2001). Similar to post-modern narratives, there is no one single version of a joint-use library; rather, each library user creates his/her own interpretation. There is no one correct, 'official' story of a joint-use library. Individual library users will use the range of services and resources on offer in a unique combination of ways to meet their individual information, learning and literary needs, thus creating their own stories or 'narratives'.

Final comments

The importance of joint-use libraries, especially their potential as an effective form of twenty-first-century library provision in many different circumstances, is not currently recognised by policy-makers or by many in the library profession. Of course they are not a universal answer, but even in communities where they are not a suitable way to meet user needs, some element of collaboration and partnership working between libraries and information services is still likely to feature, and to feature more strongly, in the future.

However, the potential of joint-use libraries will only be realised if there is credible evidence to convince those outside the sector that they can and do work. There is a need to continue to build up the evidence base that currently exists. To a large extent, previous work has focused on school-public libraries, especially those in rural areas, so there is a particular need to develop knowledge relating to other types of joint-use library in other localities in both the developed and developing worlds. This means that joint-use library staff need to evaluate their services, share problems and solutions and, above all, make sure their voice is heard by other library professionals and local, national and international policy-makers.

The future of the library profession lies in collaboration and cooperation with each other and with other professions, and, as has been said before, joint-use libraries are 'the ultimate form of co-operation' (Bundy, 2003). Other libraries therefore have much to learn from the work being done by their colleagues in joint-use libraries: the innovative models of service provision they are designing; new types of partnership working they are involved in; and the novel ways of engaging with users and non-users which they are developing. Joint-use libraries should not be seen as a novelty or trivial form of library provision, but as pioneering libraries which point to the way in which all libraries should be looking to develop in the twenty-first century.

Notes

1. For example, see the case study of Oak Park in Chapter 3.
2. See www.kitengesalibrary.org/kclhome.htm.
3. See www.teachernet.gov.uk/wholeschool/extendedschools/.

Appendix I
Joint-use libraries featured in this book

Name	Partners	URL
African-American Research Library and Cultural Center, Florida, USA	Broward County Library	www.broward.org/library/aarlcc.htm
Almedalsbiblioteket, Sweden	Public library of Visby Gotland University Library	http://almedalsbibliot eket.se/
Alvin Sherman Library, Research, and Information Technology Center, Florida, USA	Broward County Board of County Commissioners Nova Southeastern University	www.nova.edu/library/main/
Ardnamurchan Library, UK	Ardnamurchan High School Highland Libraries	www.sunartcentre.org/library.htm
Blackburn Connected, West Lothian, UK	West Lothian Library Services and Customer Services	www.westlothian.gov.uk/sitecontent/libraries/blackburnlib
Bolton Libraries, UK	Bolton PCT Children's Information Service Tourist information service Local schools	www.bolton.gov.uk/portal/page?_pageid=367,128829&_dad=portal 92&_schema=PORTAL 92
The Bridge, Glasgow, UK	John Wheatley College Glasgow Libraries, Information and Learning	www.glasgow.gov.uk/en/Residents/Libraries/Librarylocations/libraryatthebridge.htm

Name	Partners	URL
Cheadle Library, Staffordshire, UK	Staffordshire Library and Information Service Staffordshire Moorlands District Council	www.staffordshire.gov .uk/leisure/libraries/ branchlibraries/ CheadleLibrary/ CheadleLibrary.htm
Charles Darwin University Library, Alice Springs Campus, Australia	Charles Darwin University (formed through merger of Centralian College and Northern Territory University) A secondary school	www.cdu.edu.au/ library/
DBC/UCF Joint-use Library, Florida, USA	Daytona Beach Community College University of Central Florida	http://library.ucf.edu/ BranchCampuses/ Daytona/library services.asp http://go.dbcc.edu/ library/
Dr Martin Luther King Jr Library, San José, California, USA	San José State University Library San José public library system	www.sjlibrary.org/index .htm
Gipsyville Library and Multipurpose Centre, Hull, UK	Hull Libraries Pickering and Newington Development Association (PANDA)	www.hullcc.gov.uk/ portal/page?_pageid= 221,93208&_dad=por tal&_schema=PORTAL &p_display_mode=LIB DTLS&p_id=26
Health Library, Stoke-on-Trent, UK	Keele University Stoke-on-Trent NHS	www.keele.ac.uk/ depts/li/hl/
Kitengesa Community Library, Uganda	Kitengesa comprehensive secondary school Local community	www.kitengesalibrary .org/kclliteracyresearch .htm
Metropolitan State University/Dayton's Bluff Branch Library, Minnesota, USA	Metropolitan State University St Paul Public Libraries	www.metrostate.edu/ library/index.html www.sppl.org/locations/ daytonsbluff.html

Name	Partners	URL
Moss Side Powerhouse Library, Manchester, UK	Manchester Libraries	www.manchester.gov .uk/site/scripts/ documents_info.php? categoryID=1014& documentID=812
Mount Barker Community Library, Australia	District Council of Mount Barker TAFESA	www.tafe.sa.edu.au/ Campuses/Campus List/MountBarker Campus/Library/tabid/ 972/Default.aspx
National and University Library of Iceland	National Library of Iceland University of Iceland	www.bok.hi.is/id/ 1011633
North City Library, Manchester, UK	Manchester Libraries Manchester College of Arts and Technology	www.manchester.gov .uk/site/scripts/ documents_info.php? categoryID=1014& documentID=820
North Regional/BCC Library, Florida, USA	Broward County Library Broward Community College	www.browardlibrary .org/branches/nr.htm
Oldham Library and Lifelong Learning Centre, Oldham, UK	Oldham Libraries University of Huddersfield	www.oldham.gov.uk/ community/libraries/ oldham-library.htm
Papworth Library, Cambridgeshire, UK	Cambridgeshire Libraries and Information Service Papworth Trust	www.cambridgeshire .gov.uk/leisure/libraries /directory/papworth_ library.htm
Rockingham Regional Campus Community Library, Australia	City of Rockingham, Challenger TAFE Murdoch University	www.rocklibrary .murdoch.edu.au/ about.html
Sunshine Library, Wakefield, UK	Wakefield Libraries Sure Start	www.wakefield.gov.uk/ CultureAndLeisure/ Libraries/LocalLibraries/ SunshineLibrary/ default.htm
UHI Millennium Institute, UK	University of the Highlands and Islands Various schools, libraries and community venues	www.uhi.ac.uk/

Name	Partners	URL
West Community Library at St Petersburg College, Florida, USA	St Petersburg Public Library System St Petersburg College	www.splibraries.org/West.htm
Wootton Fields, Northamptonshire, UK	Northamptonshire County Council Caroline Chisholm School	www.northamptonshire.gov.uk/Leisure/Libraries/Public/woollib.htm
Zentrum für Information und Bildung, Germany		www.unna.de/zib/

Appendix II
Single-sector library standards

Academic libraries (universities and colleges)

- *Guidelines for Colleges: Recommendations for Learning Resources.* London: Colleges of Further and Higher Education Group of CILIP (UK), 2005.
- *Space Requirements for Academic Libraries and Learning Resource Centres.* Andrew McDonald. London: SCONUL, 1996.
- *Standards for Libraries in Higher Education.* Association of College and Research Libraries (USA), 2004 (www.ala.org/ala/acrl/acrlstandards/standardsguidelines.htm).

Public libraries

International

- *The Public Library Service: IFLA/UNESCO Guidelines for Development.* IFLA Section on Public Libraries, 2001 (www.ifla.org/VII/s8/proj/publ97.pdf).

Australia

- *Standards, Guidelines and Benchmarks for Public Library Services in Australia and Overseas: A Guide to Resources*, ALIA Public Libraries Reference Group, 2005 (http://alia.org.au/governance/committees/public.libraries/).

New Zealand

- *Standards for New Zealand Public Libraries*, 6th edn. Wellington: Library and Information Association of New Zealand, 2004.

UK

- *A Safe Place for Children.* CILIP, 2005 (www.cilip .org.uk/NR/rdonlyres/97A1DE77-94DC-4C69-8761-7C5B227B5F20/0/ASafePlaceforChildrenmay05.doc).

- *Standards for the Public Library Service in Scotland.* Convention of Scottish Local Authorities. Edinburgh: HMSO, 1995.

- *Public Library Service Standards.* Department for Culture Media and Sport (DCMS), 2001, revised 2004, 2006 (www.culture.gov.uk/Reference_library/Publications/ archive_2006/pls_standards06.htm).

- *Public Libraries.* House of Commons Committee on Culture, Media and Sport, Third Report Session 2004–5 (HC81) (www.publications.parliament.uk/pa/cm200405/ cmselect/cmcumeds/81/81i.pdf).

- *Comprehensive, Efficient and Modern Public Libraries for Wales: Standards and Monitoring.* National Assembly for Wales, 2001 (http://new.wales.gov.uk/topics/cultureandsport/ museumsarchiveslibraries/cymalL4/libraries_local/644406).

USA

- *HAPLR Ratings* (Hennen's American Public Library Ratings), annual. Racine, WI: haplr-index.com (www.haplr-index.com/index.html).

There are standards for some states, for example:

- Colorado Public Library Standards. Colorado State Library, 2005 (www.cde.state.co.us/cdelib/Standards/pdf/COPublicLibraryStandardsFactSheet.pdf).
- *Wisconsin Public Library Standards*, 4th edn. Wisconsin Department of Public Instruction, 2005 (http://dpi.state.wi.us/pld/standard.html).

Library services for children and young people

International

- *Guidelines for Children's Libraries*. IFLA Libraries for Children and Young Adults Section, 2003 (www.ifla.org/VII/s10/pubs/ChildrensGuidelines.pdf).
- *Guidelines for Library Services for Young Adults*. IFLA Libraries for Children and Young Adults Section, 2001 (www.ifla.org/VII/s10/pubs/guidelines-e.pdf).

UK

- *Children and Young People: Library Association Guidelines for Public Library Services*. CILIP Youth Libraries Group. London: Library Association Publishing, 1997.

School libraries

International

- *IFLA/UNESCO School Library Guidelines.* IFLA School Libraries and Resource Centers Section, 2002 (www.ifla.org/VII/s11/pubs/school-guidelines.htm).

UK

- *CILIP Guidelines for Secondary School Libraries.* L. Barrett and J. Douglas (eds), 2nd edn. London: Facet, 2004.

- *CILIP Primary School Guidelines.* CILIP, updated 2004 (www.cilip.org.uk/professionalguidance/sections/young people/primaryguidelines.htm).

- *Standards for School Library Resource Services in Scotland: A Framework for Developing Services.* Convention of Scottish Local Authorities. Edinburgh: COSLA, 1999.

USA

Similarly to public libraries, there are guidelines for individual states. Some examples include:

- *Standards and Guidelines for Strong School Libraries.* Sacramento, CA: California School Library Association, 2004.

- *Texas School Libraries: Standards, Resources, Services, and Students' Performance.* Texas State Library and Archives Commission, 2001 (www.tsl.state.tx.us/ld/pubs/ schlibsurvey/survey.doc).

References

Aaron, Shirley (1980) *A Study of Combined School-Public Libraries*. Chicago: American Library Association.

Alberta Municipal Affairs and Housing (2003) 'Standards for member libraries with Alberta's regional library systems'; available at: *www.municipalaffairs.gov.ab.ca/documents/lcvss/Standards.pdf* (accessed: 11 November 2007).

Alemna, A. Anaba (1995) 'Community libraries: an alternative to public libraries in Africa', *Library Review*, 44(7): 40–4.

Alvin Sherman Library, Research, and Information Technology Center (2006) 'Patron portals'; available at: *www.nova.edu/library/portal/* (accessed: 17 September 2007).

American Library Association (2000) 'Twelve ways libraries are good for the country'; available at: *www.ala.org/ala/alonline/selectedarticles/12wayslibraries.cfm* (accessed: 10 November 2007).

American Library Association Committee on Post-War Planning (1945) *School Libraries for Today and Tomorrow: Functions and Standards*. Chicago: American Library Association.

Amey, Larry J. (1984) *Joint Use Library Evaluation: A Plan for Assessing the Performance and Progress of Joint Use Libraries*. Adelaide: Education Department of South Australia.

Apt Partnership (1995) *The Apt Review: A Review of Library and Information Co-operation in the UK and Republic of Ireland for the Library and Information Co-operation Council (LINC)*. Sheffield: LINC.

Audit Commission (2002) 'Building better library services'; available at: *www.audit-commission.gov.uk/reports/NATIONAL-REPORT.asp?CategoryID=&ProdID=9D0A0DD1-3BF9-4c52-9112-67D520E7C0AB* (accessed: 10 November 2007).

Australian Library and Information Association (2002) 'Statement on joint-use libraries'; available at: *http://alia.org.au/policies/joint-use.html* (accessed: 14 October 2007).

Australian Library and Information Association (2006) 'Statement on libraries and literacies'; available at: *www.alia.org.au/policies/library.literacy.html* (accessed: 10 January 2007).

Barton, David, Brookes, Joanna and Ryan, Rebecca (2007) 'Sharing spaces, strengthening services: a case study of public and academic library cohabitation', in Bundy, Alan (ed.) *Joint Use Libraries, An International Conference, Proceedings*. Adelaide: Auslib Press, pp. 99–103.

Bauer, Patricia T. (2007) 'Changing places: personnel issues of a joint use library in transition', in Bundy, Alan (ed.) *Joint Use Libraries, An International Conference, Proceedings*. Adelaide: Auslib Press, pp. 64–7.

Berger, Christopher (2000) *Public and School Libraries: Issues and Options of Joint Use Facilities and Cooperative Use Agreements*. Sacramento, CA: California State Library.

Beveridge, Richard (2007) 'Building effective public private partnerships: the Wootton Fields Library', in Bundy, Alan (ed.) *Joint Use Libraries, An International Conference, Proceedings*. Adelaide: Auslib Press, pp. 124–5.

Bolton Council (2006a) 'The art of consultation final report'; available at: *www.bolton.gov.uk/pls/portal92/docs/52654.PDF* (accessed: 30 October 2007).

Bolton Council (2006b) 'Shaping future services'; available at: *www.bolton.gov.uk/pls/portal92/docs/PAGE/CHIEF_EXECUTIVES_DEPARTMENT/STRATEGIC_PROJECTS/BOLTON_PLAN_2006-09/ShapingFutureServices.htm* (accessed: 17 September 2007).

Bozeman, Dee and Owens, Rachael (2007) 'A joint use library in central Florida USA: challenges and success', in Bundy, Alan (ed.) *Joint Use Libraries, An International Conference, Proceedings.* Adelaide: Auslib Press, pp. 31–5.

Brough, Irene (2007) 'Blackburn Connected: the customer is never in the wrong place', in Bundy, Alan (ed.) *Joint Use Libraries, An International Conference, Proceedings.* Adelaide: Auslib Press, pp. 142–6.

Broward County Board of County Commissioners (undated:a) 'The African-American Research Library and Cultural Center'; available at: *www.broward.org/library/aarlcc.htm* (accessed: 10 October 2007).

Broward County Board of County Commissioners (undated:b) 'Focus on friends – Friends of North Regional/BCC Library'; available at: *www.broward.org/library/bcl_fnorthreg.htm* (accessed: 16 October 2007).

Buiskool, Bert-Jan, Grijpstra, Douwe, van Kan, Carlos, van Lakerveld, Jaap and den Oudendammer, Frowine (2005) 'Developing local learning centres and learning partnerships as part of member states' targets for reaching the Lisbon goals in the field of education and training. A study of the current situation'; available at: *http://ec.europa.eu/education/policies/2010/studies/locallearning.pdf* (accessed: 18 August 2007).

Bundy, Alan (1997) 'Widening client horizons: joint use public libraries, progress and potential', paper presented at 'Creating tomorrow today: can you imagine...', Public Libraries Section and Reference and Information Services Section Conference, Brisbane, 9–12 November; available at: *www.library.unisa.edu.au/about/papers/widen.pdf* (accessed: 4 November 2007).

Bundy, Alan (2003) 'Joint-use libraries – the ultimate form of cooperation', in McCabe, Gerard and Kennedy, James (eds) *Planning the Modern Public Library Building.* Westport, CT: Libraries Unlimited, pp. 129–48.

Bundy, Alan (2004) 'Places of connection: new public and academic library buildings in Australia and New Zealand', paper presented at Library Buildings Conference, Bournemouth, 5–6 February; available at: *www .bournemouth.gov.uk/Library/PDF/Leisure/Libraries/ Places%20of%20connection.pdf* (accessed: 17 November 2007).

Bundy, Alan (2007) 'Widening horizons: joint use libraries and South Australia's unique system of rural school community libraries', in Bundy, Alan (ed.) *Joint Use Libraries, An International Conference, Proceedings.* Adelaide: Auslib Press, pp. 3–15.

Bundy, Alan and Amey, Larry (2006) 'Libraries like no others: evaluating the performance and progress of joint use libraries', *Library Trends*, 54(4): 501–18.

Cabinet Office (2005) *Transformational Government: Enabled by Technology*; available at: *www.cio.gov.uk/ transformational_government/strategy* (accessed: 10 November 2007).

Cambridgeshire Libraries & Information Service (2005) 'Papworth Library profile'; available at: *www.cambridgeshire .gov.uk/NR/rdonlyres/98D477B0-6C89-4737-ACBB- B74087C41839/0/papworth_profile.pdf* (accessed: 20 September 2007).

Centre for Economic & Social Inclusion (undated) 'Social inclusion'; available at: *www.cesi.org.uk/kbdocs/socinc.doc* (accessed: 10 November 2007).

CILIP (2002a) 'Making a difference – innovation and diversity, final report of the Social Inclusion Executive Advisory Group'; available at: *www.cilip.org.uk/professional guidance/socialinclusion/default.htm* (accessed: 15 October 2007).

CILIP (2002b) 'Start with the child, report of the CILIP Working Group on Library Provision for Children and Young People'; available at: *www.cilip.org.uk/NR/ rdonlyres/D94ED35A-81DB-4421-9815-74F2B454A7AB/ 0/startwiththechild.pdf* (accessed: 4 November 2007).

Committee of Inquiry into Public Libraries (1976) *Public Libraries in Australia.* Canberra: Australian Government Publication Service.

Committee on Public Libraries Housed in Schools (2006) *Public Libraries Housed in School Facilities Report.* Alberta: Alberta Community Development.

Council for Museums, Libraries and Archives (2004) *Disability Portfolio*; available at: *www.mla.gov.uk/ website/policy/Diversity/Disability_Portfolio/* (accessed: 27 December 2007).

Dalton, Pete, Mynott, Glen, Nankivell, Clare and Reardon, Denis (1999) *Cross-sectoral Mobility in the LIS Profession,* Library and Information Commission Research Report 19; available at: *www.ebase.bcu.ac.uk/cirtarchive/publications/ Cross_LIS.pdf* (accessed: 4 November 2007).

Dave, R.H. (1976) *Foundations of Lifelong Education.* Oxford: Pergamon.

Dent, Valeda Frances (2006) 'Modelling the rural community library: characteristics of the Kitengesa Library in rural Uganda', *New Library World*, 107(1220/1): 16–30.

Department for Culture, Media and Sport (2003) *Framework for the Future: Libraries, Learning and Information in the Next Decade*; available at: *www.culture.gov.uk/Reference_library/Publications/archive_2003/framework_future.htm* (accessed: 4 November 2007).

Department for Culture, Media and Sport (2006) *Public Library Service Standards*; available at: *www.culture.gov.uk/Reference_library/Publications/archive_2006/pls_standards06.htm* (accessed: 5 May 2007).

Department for Education and Skills (2003) *The Future of Higher Education*; available at: *www.dfes.gov.uk/hegateway/uploads/White%20Pape.pdf* (accessed: 10 November 2007).

Department for Education and Skills (2004a) *Every Child Matters: The Next Steps*; available at: *www.everychildmatters.gov.uk/_files/A39928055378AF27E9122D734BF10F74.pdf* (accessed: 11 November 2007).

Department for Education and Skills (2004b) *Five Year Strategy for Children and Learners*; available at: *www.dfes.gov.uk/publications/5yearstrategy* (accessed: 10 November 2007).

Department for Education and Skills (2004c) *School Library Self-evaluation Frameworks*; available at: *www.teachernet.gov.uk/docbank/index.cfm?id=6616* (accessed: 4 November 2007).

Department for Work and Pensions (2006) 'Making a difference: tackling poverty – a progress report'; available at: *www.dwp.gov.uk/publications/dwp/2006/poverty/tackling-poverty.pdf* (accessed: 10 November 2007).

Department of Education and Science (1970) *The Chance to Share*, Circular 2/70. London: DES.

Department of Health (2005) 'Commissioning a patient-led NHS'; available at: *www.dh.gov.uk/en/Publicationsandstatistics/Publications/PublicationsPolicyAndGuidance/DH_4116716* (accessed: 26 December 2007).

Dewe, Michael (2006) *Planning Public Library Buildings. Concepts and Issues for the Librarian.* Aldershot: Ashgate.

Dornseif, Karen A. (2001) 'Joint use libraries: balancing autonomy and cooperation', *Resource Sharing and Information Networks*, 15(12): 103–15.

Dorrington, Linda (2006) 'Health libraries as joint use libraries: serving medical practitioners and students', *Library Trends*, 54(4): 596–606.

Dwyer, Jim (1978) *Cooperation or Compromise: School Community Libraries in Australia. Report to the Commonwealth Schools Commission.* Canberra: Commonwealth Schools Commission.

EBLIDA (2001) 'EBLIDA statement to the European Commission memorandum on lifelong learning'; available at: *www.eblida.org/uploads/eblida/13/1167686623.pdf* (accessed: 16 October 2007).

Evidence Base (2006) 'evalued: an evaluation toolkit for e-library developments'; available at: *www.evalued.bcu .ac.uk/* (accessed: 11 November 2007).

Evidence Base (2007) 'Platt Bridge Community Library, Wigan'; available at: *www.ebase.bcu.ac.uk/dualuse/ featured.htm* (accessed: 4 November 2007).

Fairman, Roger (2007) 'Connections, individuals, raising aspirations: Worcester's unique joint use library and history centre project', in Bundy, Alan (ed.) *Joint Use Libraries, An International Conference, Proceedings.* Adelaide: Auslib Press, pp. 111–13.

Fenwick, Sara (1966) *School and Children's Libraries in Australia.* Melbourne: Cheshire.

Fenwick, Sara (1975) 'Public and school libraries in community library movements', *The Teacher Librarian*, 39: 21–6.

Fitzgibbons, S.A. (2000) 'School and public library relationships: essential ingredients in implementing educational reforms and improving student learning',

School Library Media Research, 3; available at: *www.ala.org/aasl/SLMR/vol3/relationships/relationships_main.htm* (accessed: 17 September 2007).

Hall, Lorraine and Curry, Sally (2000) *The SAILS Project: A Working Guide to Cross-sectoral Co-operation Supporting Lifelong Learning and Staff Development*, Library and Information Commission Research Report 36. London: British Library.

Hamblin, Deb (2007) 'Innovation, experimentation and persistence: the success factors of an Australian tripartite library', in Bundy, Alan (ed.) *Joint Use Libraries, An International Conference, Proceedings*. Adelaide: Auslib Press, pp. 71–8.

Hansson, Joacim (2006) 'Just collaboration or really something else? On joint-use libraries and normative institutional change with two examples from Sweden', *Library Trends*, 54(4): 549–68.

Hansson, Joacim (2007) 'New document environments and institutional identities: joint use libraries at the crossroads between the physical and the digital library', in Bundy, Alan (ed.) *Joint Use Libraries, An International Conference, Proceedings*. Adelaide: Auslib Press, pp. 79–83.

Hardman, Lesley and Melmoth, Ann (2007) 'Partnerships mean progress', in Bundy, Alan (ed.) *Joint Use Libraries, An International Conference, Proceedings*. Adelaide: Auslib Press, pp. 16–19.

Haycock, Ken (1979) 'Combined school/public libraries: some basic considerations', in Amey, Larry J. (ed.) *The Canadian School-housed Public Library*. London: Vine Press, pp. 49–52.

HEFCE (2006) 'Shared services: the benefits for higher education institutions', Circular Letter No. 20/2006; available at: *www.hefce.ac.uk/pubcirclets/2006/cl20_06/* (accessed: 10 November 2007).

Hillenbrand, Candy (2005) 'A place for all: social capital at the Mount Barker Community Library, South Australia'. *Australasian Public Libraries and Information*, 18(2): 41–60.

Hopkins, Alison and Turner, Shad (2006) 'Synergy in the north: school and public libraries join forces in the NWT', *School Libraries in Canada*, 25(3): 8–11.

IFLA (1996) 'Act on Library Services, Swedish Code of Statutes – SFS 1996:1596'; available at: *www.ifla.org/V/cdoc/swedish.htm* (accessed: 10 November 2007).

IFLA (2001) 'The public library service: the IFLA/UNESCO guidelines for development'; available at: *www.ifla.org/VII/s8/proj/publ97.pdf* (accessed: 10 November 2007).

IFLA/UNESCO (1994) 'Public library manifesto'; available at: *www.unesco.org/webworld/libraries/manifestos/libraman.html* (accessed: 11 November 2007).

IFLA/UNESCO (1999) *IFLA/UNESCO School Library Manifesto, The School Library in Teaching and Learning for All*; available at: *www.ifla.org/VII/s11/pubs/manifest.htm* (accessed: 26 December 2007).

Iver Community Libraries (2007) 'Iver Community Libraries website'; available at: *www.ivercommunitylibraries.org.uk/* (accessed: 14 January 2007).

Jackson, Hilary (2007) 'Staffordshire's one stop shops', in Bundy, Alan (ed.) *Joint Use Libraries, An International Conference, Proceedings*. Adelaide: Auslib Press, pp. 140–1.

Jarvis, Peter, Holford, John and Griffin, Colin (1998) *The Theory and Practice of Learning*. London: Kogan Page.

Jones, Arthur (1977) 'Dual purpose libraries: some experience in England', *School Librarian*, 25(4): 311–18.

Jordan, Anne (2005) 'Double booking; a city and a university sharing a library? It's not easy, but San José is doing it', *Governing*, 18(11): 44–9.

Karp, R.S. (1996) 'The literature of joint-use libraries', in Williams, D.E. and Garten, E.D. (eds) *Advances in Library Administration and Organization*. Greenwich, CT: JAI Press, pp. 227–71.

Keane, Mary (2007) 'The family way: meeting local needs in Bolton', in Bundy, Alan (ed.) *Joint Use Libraries, An International Conference, Proceedings*. Adelaide: Auslib Press, pp. 118–23.

Kearney, Catherine (2007) 'Collaborative communities: new service delivery models for lifelong learning in Scotland', in Bundy, Alan (ed.) *Joint Use Libraries, An International Conference, Proceedings*. Adelaide: Auslib Press, pp. 136–9.

Kempson, Elaine (1986) 'Information for self-reliance and self-determination: the role of community information services', *IFLA Journal*, 12(3): 182–91.

Kifer, Ruth E. (2007) 'The Dr Martin Luther King Jr Library: public policy in action in Silicon Valley USA', in Bundy, Alan (ed.) *Joint Use Libraries, An International Conference, Proceedings*. Adelaide: Auslib Press, pp. 104–10.

Kitengesa Community Library (2004) 'Kitengesa Community Library'; available at: *www.kitengesalibrary.org/kclhome.htm* (accessed: 15 October 2007).

Knowles, Malcolm S. (1990) *The Adult Learner: A Neglected Species*, 4th edn. Houston, TX: Gulf Publishing.

Koenig, Michael D.E. and Safford, Herbert D. (1984) 'Myths, misconceptions and management', *Library Journal*, 109(17): 1897–902.

Lacroix, Eve-Marie and Backus, Joyce L.F. (2006) 'Organizing electronic information to serve the needs of health practitioners and customers', *Library Trends*, 54(4): 607–19.

Lance, Keith Curry, Rodney, Marcia J. and Hamilton-Pennell, Christine (2002) 'How school librarians help kids achieve standards, the second Colorado study';

available at: *www.lrs.org/documents/lmcstudies/CO/execsumm.pdf* (accessed: 4 August 2007).

Le Roux, Sophia and Hendrikz, Francois (2006) 'Joint use libraries: implementing a pilot community-school library project in a remote rural area in South Africa', *Library Trends*, 54(4): 620–39.

Leicester City Council (undated) 'Age Concern Library', available at: *www.leicester.gov.uk/index.asp?pgid=43504* (accessed: 14 October 2007).

Library and Information Commission (2000) 'Empowering the learning community', available at: *www.mla.gov.uk/action/learnacc/emplearn00.asp* (accessed: 10 November 2007).

London Councils (2006) 'Community engagement – what is it and why is it important?', available at: *www.londoncouncils.gov.uk/doc.asp?doc=16452&CAT=2195* (accessed: 15 October 2007).

MacDougall, Harriett (2007) 'A five year assessment of a large joint use library in southeast Florida USA: a case study', in Bundy, Alan (ed.) *Joint Use Libraries, An International Conference. Proceedings.* Adelaide: Auslib Press, pp. 93–8.

MacInnes, Neil and Long, Eunice (2007) 'Partnership and collocation: the Mancunian way', in Bundy, Alan (ed.) *Joint Use Libraries, An International Conference, Proceedings.* Adelaide: Auslib Press, pp. 131–5.

Martins, Ana Bela (2007) 'The Portuguese School Libraries Network Program: a net built in partnership', in Bundy, Alan (ed.) *Joint Use Libraries, An International Conference. Proceedings.* Adelaide: Auslib Press, pp. 61–3.

McNicol, Sarah (2003) 'Dual use public and school libraries in the UK', available at: *www.ebase.uce.ac.uk/docs/Dual_use_libraries_supplementary_report.doc* (accessed: 4 November 2007).

McNicol, Sarah and Dalton, Pete (2003) 'Public libraries: supporting the learning process', available at: *www.ebase .bcu.ac.uk/docs/public_libraries_learning_report.doc* (accessed: 10 November 2007).

McNicol, Sarah, Matthews, Graham, Kane, David, Lancaster, Katy, Thebridge, Stella and Dalton, Pete (2002) 'Collaboration between libraries and education: supporting the learner', available at: *www.ebase.bcu.ac .uk/cirtarchive/projects/past/collaboration.htm* (accessed: 11 November 2007).

Miller, William and Pellen, Rita M. (2001) *Joint-use Libraries*. Binghamton: Haworth Information Press.

Morden, Sandra (2003) 'Cooperation between public libraries and schools in Canada', available at: *www.library.on.ca/links/clearinghouse/administration/ CELPLO.pdf* (accessed: 10 November 2007).

Mostert, B.J. (1998) 'Community libraries: the concept and its application – with particular reference to a South African library system', *International Information and Library Review*, 30: 71–85.

Murphy, Patricia F. (ed.) (1999) *Learners, Learning and Assessment*. London: Paul Chapman.

Museums, Libraries and Archives Council (2004) *Inspiring Learning for All*, available at: *www.inspiringlearning forall.gov.uk/* (accessed: 10 November 2007).

Museums, Libraries and Archives Council (2007) 'A blueprint for excellence', available at: *www.mla.gov.uk/ resources/assets/I/blueprint_v2_11233.pdf* (accessed: 17 September 2007).

Mynott, Glyn, Nankivell, Clare, Foster, William and Elkin, Judith (1998) 'People flows: an investigation of the cross-use of publicly-funded libraries', available at: *www .ebase.bcu.ac.uk/cirtarchive/projects/past/people_flows.htm* (accessed: 10 November 2007).

National Commission on Libraries and Information Science (NCLIS) (1975) *Toward a National Program for Library and Information Services: Goals for Action*. Washington, DC: Superintendent of Documents, US Government Printing Office; available at: *www.nclis.gov/info/Towarda NationalProgramforLibraryandInformationServices-1975.pdf* (accessed: 26 December 2007).

National Education Association – Library Department (1899) 'Report of the Committee on the Relations of Public Libraries to Public Schools', in *NEA Proceedings*. Washington, DC: NEA, pp. 452–529.

National Literacy Trust (2007) 'Case study: The Sunshine (Sure Start) Library, Wakefield'; available at: *www .literacytrust.org.uk/socialinclusion/earlyyears/sunshine .html* (accessed: 14 October 2007).

Ndlovu, Jackson (2007) Personal communication from director of library services, Natural History Museum, Bulawayo, Zimbabwe, 31 July.

New Jersey Association of School Librarians, New Jersey Library Association and New Jersey State Library (2003) 'School/public library joint use facility standards'; available at: *www.emanj.org/documents/Guidelinesfor JointSchool-PublicLibraries_000.pdf* (accessed: 26 December 2007).

Nova Scotia Economic Development (2006) 'Opportunities for sustainable prosperity 2006'; available at: *www.gov .ns.ca/econ/ofsp/docs/Opportunities_For_Sustainable_ Prosperity_2006.pdf* (accessed: 15 October 2007).

Office of the Deputy Prime Minister (2003) 'Community cohesion and neighbourhood renewal', Factsheet 15; available at: *www.creatingexcellence.org.uk/uploads/ factsheet14_cohesionandrenewal.pdf* (accessed: 26 December 2007).

Oldenburg, Ray (1989) *The Great Good Place: Cafes, Coffee Shops, Community Centers, Beauty Parlors, General Stores, Bars, Hangouts and How They Get You Through the Day*. New York: Paragon House.

Oldham Council (undated) 'Oldham Library & Lifelong Learning Centre'; available at: *www.oldham.gov .uk/community/libraries/oldham-library.htm* (accessed: 20 September 2007).

Parker, Sandra, Waterston, Ken, Michaluk, Gerald and Rickard, Louise (2002) 'Neighbourhood renewal and social inclusion: the role of museums, archives and libraries'; available at: *www.mla.gov.uk/resources/assets// N/neighbourhood_pdf_5678.pdf* (accessed: 10 November 2007).

Philip, A. (1980) 'Organization and management of rural (village) libraries', *Maktaba*, 7(2): 143–55.

Ping, Ke (2001) 'Toward continual reform: progress in academic libraries in China' (translated by Sha Li Zhang), *College and Research Libraries*, 63(2); available at: *http://news.ala.org/ala/acrl/acrlpubs/crljournal/backissues 2002b/march02/zhang.pdf* (accessed: 11 November 2007).

Public Library Association Committee on Standards for Work with Young Adults in Public Libraries (1960) *Young Adult Services in the Public Library*. Chicago: American Library Association.

Queensland Government (2005) 'Joint-use public/school library standards'; available at: *www.slq.qld.gov.au/info/ publib/policy/guidelines/thirteen#stand* (accessed: 11 November 2007).

Quinlan, Nora J. and Tuñón, Johanna (2005) 'Providing reference in a joint-use library', *Internet Reference Services Quarterly*, 9(1/2): 111–28.

Ray, Kathlin L. (2001) 'The postmodern library in an age of assessment', paper presented to ARCL Tenth National

Conference; available at: *www.ala.org/ala/acrl/acrlevents/ kray.pdf* (accessed: 11 November 2007).

Resource (2000) *Open to All? The Public Library and Social Exclusion. Volume 1: Overview and Conclusions*, Library and Information Commission Research Report 84. London: LIC.

Richmond, Sue (2007) 'Staffing and management of joint use libraries: a case study', in Bundy, Alan (ed.) *Joint Use Libraries, An International Conference, Proceedings.* Adelaide: Auslib Press, pp. 68–70.

Roach, Patrick and Morrison, Marlene (1998) *Public Libraries, Ethnic Diversity and Citizenship*, British Library Research and Innovation Report 76. London: British Library Research and Innovation Centre.

Schamber, Linda (1990) 'The role of libraries in literacy education', *ERIC Digest*; available at: *www .ericdigests.org/pre-9219/role.htm* (accessed: 10 November 2007).

School Library Association (1972) *School Libraries – Their Planning and Equipment.* London: SLA.

School Library Association (2007) 'Dual use libraries'; available at: *www.sla.org.uk/pol-dual-use-libraries.php* (accessed: 11 January 2007).

SCONUL (2007) 'SCONUL statistics'; available at: *www .sconul.ac.uk/statistics* (accessed: 11 November 2007).

Scottish Executive (2003a) *The Lifelong Learning Strategy for Scotland*; available at: *www.scotland.gov.uk/Publications/ 2003/02/16308/17750* (accessed: 20 October 2007).

Scottish Executive (2003b) 'School opens in Ardnamurchan'; available at: *www.scotland.gov.uk/News/Releases/2003/ 06/3617* (accessed: 10 November 2007).

Scottish Executive (2004) *Building a Better Scotland*; available at: *www.scotland.gov.uk/Publications/2004/11/ 20318/47372* (accessed: 20 October 2007).

Scottish Executive (2007) 'Efficient government'; available at: *www.scotland.gov.uk/Topics/Government/Public ServiceReform/efficientgovernment* (accessed: 20 October 2007).

Shoemaker, Adam, Allison, Janelle, Gum, Kingsley, Harmoni, Rose, Lindfield, Mike, Nolan, Marguerite and Stedman, Lawrence (2000) *Multi-Partner Campuses: The Future of Australian Higher Education?* Canberra: Department of Education, Training and Youth Affairs.

SJLibrary.org (2007a) 'Dr. Martin Luther King Jr. Library vision'; available at: *www.sjlibrary.org/about/vision/index.htm* (accessed: 7 November 2007).

SJLibrary.org (2007b) 'Paths to lifelong learning'; available at: *www.sjlibrary.org/gateways/index.htm* (accessed: 17 September 2007).

Spelthorne Borough Council (2006) 'Sunbury Citizens Advice Bureau moves to library'; available at: *www.spelthorne.gov.uk/print/nws_06_cab.htm* (accessed: 18 November 2007).

State Library of Iowa (2006) 'Is a combined school/public library right for your community?'; available at: *www.statelibraryofiowa.org/ld/combined-sch-pl/guide* (accessed: 10 November 2007).

Stone, Sally (1979) 'A marriage in Bala Cynwyd', *Library Journal Special Report 9: Making Co-operation Work*: 16–20.

Sumner, Sonia and Mamtora, Jayshree (2007) 'A joint use library in the red centre of Australia', in Bundy, Alan (ed.) *Joint Use Libraries, An International Conference, Proceedings.* Adelaide: Auslib Press, pp. 20–4.

Svensson, Christina, Hamilton, Cecilia and Hagberg, Leif (2007) 'Three joint use library projects and the Combilib library network', in Bundy, Alan (ed.) *Joint Use Libraries,*

References

An International Conference. Proceedings. Adelaide: Auslib Press, pp. 89–92.

The Network (2006) 'What is community cohesion?', available at: *www.seapn.org.uk/communitycohesion_menu.html* (accessed: 4 August 2007).

UHI Millennium Institute (undated) 'Learning centres', available at: *www.uhi.ac.uk/learning-centres/information-for-learning-centre-students/learning-centres* (accessed: 10 November 2007).

UNESCO (2005) 'Alexandria Proclamation on Information Literacy and Lifelong Learning', available at: *http:// portal.unesco.org/ci/en/files/20891/11364818989Beacons_ of_the_Information_Society_The_Alexandria_Proclamation_ on_Information_Literacy_and_Lifelong_Learning.doc/ Beacons%2Bof%2Bthe%2BInformation%2BSociety_ %2B%2BThe%2BAlexandria%2BProclamation%2Bon% 2BInformation%2BLiteracy%2Band%2BLifelong% 2BLearning.doc* (accessed: 15 October 2007).

Van House, Nancy, Roderer, Nancy K. and Cooper, Michael D. (1983) 'Librarians: a study of supply and demand', *American Libraries*, 14(6): 361–70.

Vincent, John (2005) 'Libraries and community cohesion: a paper for the South East Museum, Library and Archive Council'; available at: *www.mlasoutheast.org.uk/assets/ documents/10005EAlibrariescommunitycohesion.pdf* (accessed: 10 November 2007).

White, Ruth M. (1963) *The School-housed Public Library: A Survey*. Chicago: American Library Association.

Wisconsin Department of Public Instruction (1998) *Combined School and Public Libraries: Guidelines for Decision-making*, 2nd edn; available at: *http://dpi .wisconsin.gov/pld/pdf/comblibs.pdf* (accessed: 11 November 2007).

Witbooi, Sally (2006) 'Setting up a joint-use library facility: testing an African model in Wesbank, Western Cape', *Innovation*, 32: 41–54.

Woolard, Wilma Lee Broughton (1980) *Combined School/Public Libraries: A Survey with Conclusions and Recommendations.* Metuchen, NJ: Scarecrow Press.

Zetterlund, Angela and Garden, Cecilia (2007) 'Why public libraries have problems sharing a vision of joint use libraries: experiences from a program concerning adult learners', in Bundy, Alan (ed.) *Joint Use Libraries, An International Conference, Proceedings*. Adelaide: Auslib Press, pp. 36–45.

Further reading

Allen, Stephen and Sandison, Peter (2007) 'Developing joint use facilities: a case study of the Scottish Borders campus from a construction process perspective', in Bundy, Alan (ed.) Joint Use Libraries, An International Conference, Proceedings. Adelaide: Auslib Press, pp. 25–30.

Amey, Larry J. (ed.) (1979) The Canadian School-housed Public Library. London: Vine Press.

Bauer, Patricia T. (2006) 'Changing places: personnel issues of a joint use library in transition', Library Trends, 54(4): 581–95.

Dalton, Pete, Hannaford, Anne and Elkin, Judith (2006) 'Joint use libraries as successful strategic alliances', Library Trends, 54(4): 535–48.

Haycock, Ken (2006) 'Dual use libraries: guidelines for success', Library Trends, 54(4): 488–500.

HM Treasury (2004) Spending Review: Stability, Security and Opportunity for All: Investing for Britain's Long-term Future; available at: www.hm-treasury.gov.uk/spending_review/spend_sr04/report/spend_sr04_repindex.cfm (accessed: 20 October 2007).

Madsen, Anne J. and Williams, Sue D. (1994) 'Joint-use libraries: more bang for your buck', Wilson Library Bulletin, 69: 37–9.

McNamee, Patricia E. (2007) 'Standards and guidelines for public libraries housed in schools in Alberta Canada: a case study', in Bundy, Alan (ed.) Joint Use Libraries,

An International Conference, Proceedings. Adelaide: Auslib Press, pp. 84–8.

McNicol, Sarah (2006) 'What makes a joint use library a community library', *Library Trends*, 54(4): 519–34.

McNicol, Sarah (2007) 'Joint use libraries as children's libraries', in Bundy, Alan (ed.) *Joint Use Libraries, An International Conference, Proceedings*. Adelaide: Auslib Press, pp. 126–30.

McNicol, Sarah (2007) 'Platt Bridge Community Library, Wigan'; available at: *www.ebase.bcu.ac.uk/dualuse/featured.htm* (accessed: 4 November 2007).

Polyzou, Agapi-Stamoulia and Tsoli, Theodora (2007) 'Suggestions for joint use library projects in Greece: a promising solution to the advancement of information literacy', in Bundy, Alan (ed.) *Joint Use Libraries, An International Conference, Proceedings*. Adelaide: Auslib Press, pp. 46–60.

Riley, Linda and Hargreaves, Mike (2007) 'You say tomato: merging library services in the National Health Service and higher education in the UK', in Bundy, Alan (ed.) *Joint Use Libraries, An International Conference, Proceedings*. Adelaide: Auslib Press, pp. 114–17.

San José State University Library (2007) 'Being a librarian at San José State University'; available at: *www.sjlibrary.org/about/sjsu/librarian.htm* (accessed: 15 October 2007).

State of Queensland Department of Education (1996) 'Guidelines for the development of joint-use school-community libraries'; available at: *http://education.qld.gov.au/library/docs/joint-use.pdf* (accessed: 10 November 2007).

Suffolk Strategic Partnership (undated) 'Suffolk Partnership evaluation toolkit'; available at: *http://apps2.suffolk.gov.uk/cgi-bin/committee_xml.cgi?p=doc&id=1_400&format=doc* (accessed: 1 September 2007).

Sullivan, Kathy, Taylor, Warren, Barrick, Mary-Grace and Stelk, Roger (2006) 'Building the beginnings of a beautiful partnership', *Library Trends*, 54(4): 569–80.

Vincent, John (2003) 'Definitions – what is social exclusion?'; available at: *www.seapn.org.uk/documents/ Definitions.pdf* (accessed: 4 August 2007).

Index